EVANGELICAL RENEWAL
IN THE MAINLINE CHURCHES

OTHER BOOKS BY RONALD H. NASH

EVANGELICAL RENEWAL IN THE MAINLINE CHURCHES

Ronald H. Nash
EDITOR

CROSSWAY BOOKS □ WESTCHESTER, ILLINOIS
A DIVISION OF GOOD NEWS PUBLISHERS

Evangelical Renewal in the Mainline Churches. Copyright © 1987 by Ronald H. Nash. Published by Crossway Books, a division of Good News Publishers, Westchester, Illinois 60187.

First printing, 1987

Printed in the United States of America

Library of Congress Catalog Card Number 86-72380

ISBN 0-89107-431-7

To
Ardah Perry Fuller
and to the memory of
Alexander and Mabel Perry

TABLE OF CONTENTS

INTRODUCTION
Evangelical Renewal and America's Mainline Churches

O ne of the more surprising phenomena of American religion in the late twentieth century is the resurgence of an evangelical presence in the large, mainline denominations that were once thought lost to evangelicalism. This book is an account of that evangelical renewal written largely in the words of individuals who are personally involved in the work of renewal. The denominations included in this study are the largest mainline churches in the United States: the United Methodist Church, the United Presbyterian Church, the Episcopal Church, the United Church of Christ, the Disciples of Christ, the American Baptist Churches, and the largest Lutheran denominations. America's largest Protestant denomination, the Southern Baptist Convention, is not regarded as part of the mainline church group and hence is not included in this study. However, it did seem wise to include a chapter on the U.S. Roman Catholic Church because of interesting, recent developments within that fellowship.

The primary audience for this book is the group of people who should be most interested in evangelical renewal—i.e., the clergy and laypeople who want information about renewal in their own Church as well as in other mainline denominations. The book should also be helpful to members of other religious fellowships, as well as to students in college and seminary courses that deal with contemporary American religion.

An obvious first step for such a study as this is to explain the meaning of the word *evangelical*. Evangelicals are theologically orthodox in the sense that they accept the teachings of the early Christian creeds. Evangelicals believe in the Trinity, the deity of Christ, the Incarnation, the substitutionary atone-

ment, the bodily resurrection of Christ, justification by faith,
and other essential elements of historic Christianity. Evangelicals take the Bible to be their ultimate authority in matters of
faith and practice. Evangelicals have had a religious conversion
that is sometimes described by the phrase "born again." And
evangelicals are interested in leading others to the same kind of
conversion experience.

Where is baptism??

There is nothing new about this list of convictions. In fact,
until after the Civil War every mainline Church in America was
evangelical in its theology.[1] Slowly at first, the evangelical consensus in America's mainline denominations began to crumble
under the assault of liberal views from Europe that gradually
took root in mainline seminaries. The attacks were directed at
first toward the integrity and authority of Scripture. After that
important ground had been captured, the growing liberal presence in the mainline Churches began to question such essential
Christian tenets as the deity of Christ and the bodily resurrection.

In the view of evangelical scholars such as J. Gresham
Machen who was then teaching at Princeton Theological Seminary, religious modernism was not simply a variant of historic
Christianity; it was, in fact, a totally new religion that insisted
on retaining the Christian label. According to one recent discussion of the subject,

> Liberalism not only tried to undermine faith in the cardi-
> nal doctrines of the church; it was also intensely humanis-
> tic in the sense that it believed man to be essentially good
> and fully able to solve his problems and build for himself
> a better world. The liberals were characterized by their
> great faith in human progress. They seemed to be incur-
> ably optimistic. Their theology gave the impression that
> God was present in the wonderful world of science and
> technology, working for the benefit of man. They empha-
> sized the immanence of God, passing over His transcen-
> dence. They placed the religion of feeling above the au-
> thority of written revelation. They subjected the Bible to
> the judgment of reason in the way they applied historical
> and literary criticism to it, denying the possibility that
> God could reveal Himself in a supernatural way through
> the Scriptures. Thus the liberals sacrificed the Bible's au-
> thority on the altar of human reason.[2]

Theologian James Packer notes the devastating effect of liberalism on the Church's doctrine of Christ and on its view of foreign missions:

> Just as Christ differs from other men only comparatively, not absolutely, so Christianity [in the liberal view] differs from other religions not generally, but merely as the best and highest type of religion that has yet appeared. All religions are forms of the same religion, just as all men are members of the same divine family. It follows, of course, that Foreign Missions should not aim to convert from one faith to another, but rather to promote a cross-fertilizing interchange whereby each religion may be enriched through the contribution of all others.[3]

Protestant liberalism was a religion without a personal God, without a divine Savior, without an inspired Bible, and without a life-transforming conversion. By the end of the 1920s, this new religion had gained control of denominational schools, publications, mission boards, and eventually total control of the mainline denominations.

Students of America's religious history in the twentieth century will know that the complete story was actually much more complex than this brief account suggests. Theologically conservative Protestants often failed to present a united front to the liberal challenge. Some responsible conservatives were repelled by the tactics of some fundamentalists. Other theological conservatives were affected by their loyalty to the denomination. Some conservatives drew the battle lines in the wrong places.

Once effective control of a mainline Church had passed to the liberals, many conservatives pulled out of their denomination. In some cases, they joined already existing fellowships that shared essential convictions; in other instances, they formed new but obviously smaller and less influential denominations that were designed to preserve their convictions. One obvious consequence of the massive exodus of Protestant conservatives that occurred in such mainline denominations as the Northern Baptist Convention (now the American Baptist Churches) and the Presbyterian Church in the U.S.A. was even greater liberal control of those Churches.

Nothing in these words is meant as criticism of those who pulled out of their denominations or, for that matter, of those conservatives who chose to remain. Those were trying times when sincere men and women faced difficult choices with regard to their understanding of their responsibility to Christ and His Church. The point is that during the 1950s any evangelical presence within the mainline Churches was small, largely silent, and easy to ignore.

Suddenly—or so it seems—the sleeping giant of evangelicalism has begun to stir. Suddenly a number of the large, liberal, mainline Churches that were once thought lost to evangelicalism have a growing evangelical presence in their midst. In some denominations, this evangelical movement seems feeble and immature. But infants do have a way of growing up and making their presence known. In other denominations, such as the Episcopal Church or the United Presbyterian Church, it is hard to turn around without bumping into one of many evangelical renewal movements. Here and there, in little pockets, in isolated churches, the seeds of revival and renewal are beginning to sprout. Faithful pastors are proclaiming the truth of God, and people are beginning to respond. Easy access to Biblically faithful teaching and preaching on television has brought the gospel into millions of lives that fail to hear that message in their mainline Church. Religious bookstores are ready sources of helpful literature.

Another important factor must be considered in all this. Over the past ten years, the mainline Churches have lost hundreds of thousands of members along with the financial support those members used to provide. At the same time, America's conservative Churches were experiencing dramatic growth in numbers. Many understandably interpret these disparate results as the inevitable result of the different messages of different religions. Liberalism denies the importance of repentance and conversion. It is a religion without a divine Savior, without an inspired Word from God, without the hope of forgiveness in this life or eternal life in the next. For all of its problems and shortcomings, evangelicalism has something missing from liberalism: the life-transforming message of the New Testament gospel.

What are the essential elements of genuine evangelical renewal? First, of course, there must be *doctrinal renewal*. Over the past century, much mainline Christianity has lost, denied, or forgotten essential Christian beliefs. Evangelical renewal must include a concern to return those beliefs to their proper place of prominence.

But genuine evangelical renewal will also include *spiritual renewal.* This spiritual renewal will focus on conversion, on living the Christian life, on worship, and on evangelism. Evangelical renewal can hardly be present in a theologically orthodox Church that fails to challenge its people to experience God's saving grace, that ignores the proper place of worship and study of God's Word, and that fails to exhibit God's power in the lives of its people.

The rest of this book discusses the status of evangelical renewal in America's largest mainline Churches as well as in the Roman Catholic Church. The authors of these chapters provide only one perspective on renewal within their denomination. There are undoubtedly other writers who would provide a somewhat different picture. No writer claims to provide the final word either about his denomination or about the renewal movement in that Church.

Clearly the time has come for Christians to give serious attention to renewal. The chapters in this book provide a helpful starting-point both for reflection and for action.

—*Ronald H. Nash*

JAMES HEIDINGER II

is executive secretary of Good News, a Forum for Scriptural Christianity within the United Methodist Church. He also serves as editor of *Good News* magazine, for which he has also written many articles. Dr. Heidinger edited the book *Basic United Methodist Beliefs: An Evangelical View.* Dr. Heidinger holds degrees from Asbury College (B.A.), Asbury Theological Seminary (B.D., Th.M.), and Wesley Theological Seminary (D. Min.). He is a ministerial member of the East Ohio Annual Conference of the United Methodist Church.

O N E

The United Methodist Church
James Heidinger II

I n March 1967, Charles W. Keysor, a Methodist pastor in Elgin, Illinois, began publishing a small magazine for evangelicals within the Methodist Church. At the suggestion of his wife, he called it *Good News*.

Chuck, as he was known to us, had no way of knowing what was being launched that day. But twenty years later, we do. His effort to speak on behalf of the evangelical constituency within the liberal Methodist Church was the start of what has become a national movement for renewal within the second largest Protestant denomination in America.

Today Good News, known officially as a Forum for Scriptural Christianity, ministers within United Methodism as an unofficial movement for Scriptural and theological renewal. Yet some people view Good News as bad news for the United Methodist Church. They call us divisive, narrow, and intolerant. But for others, Good News is a prophetic voice calling the Church to renewed faithfulness to the gospel. For these, we provide hope and a reason for remaining within the denomination.

But not all United Methodists have chosen to stay. Over the last nineteen years the United Methodist Church has lost more than 1.8 million members, leaving our present membership at 9.15 million. To help put that in perspective, only twenty religious groups in America *have* more members than the United Methodist Church *lost* during the last nineteen years!

THE LEGACY OF LIBERALISM

One might well ask what has happened to Methodism—a denomination with such rich, evangelical roots. The warmed hearts of the Wesleys in England fanned the flames of revival that spread across the continent and beyond. The "inextinguishable blaze" made its way to America where Asbury, Coke, and others were used by God to make Methodism a dynamic and rapidly-growing Church.

Throughout the 1800s, Methodist circuit riders followed the American frontier as it moved west. They did their job so well that church historians credit them with helping civilize the "wild west."

But the period at the turn of the century, 1895-1930, was a time of turbulence and transition for the Methodist Church. Up till then, Methodists were growing, building churches, evangelizing, and establishing colleges. Suddenly winds of change were blowing within American Protestantism. And Methodism did not escape their destructive impact.

During this period, Methodist theologians and teachers drank deeply from the springs of Social Darwinism, the new science, European Rationalism, and theological modernism. Methodist leaders were euphoric about their new "Social Creed" (formulated in 1907) and the emerging Social Gospel. The new obsession of the Church was ministry to critical human needs in urban areas.

But while zeal for social ministry flourished, concern for theological matters floundered. During the first quarter of the century, Methodists viewed theology with waning interest and sometimes antipathy. Many were saying, in essence, "With such serious need in our cities, how can we bicker over something so unimportant as doctrine?"

Methodists felt they were being freed from the provincialism of orthodoxy. A new day was dawning, or so it seemed.

So, conforming to the prevailing mood, in 1916 Methodism's General Conference (the denomination's main governing body) voted to remove the Articles of Religion as a test for membership. (The Articles were a series of doctrinal definitions adopted by Wesley from the Church of England and sent to America to become the statement of orthodox Methodist doctrine.) And in 1932, the General Conference dropped the Apostles' Creed from the baptismal ritual.

So great, in fact, was the decline of interest in theology and even the abandonment of basic doctrinal tenets that some began to protest publicly this ominous trend. In 1933, Drew

University's eminent Edwin Lewis wrote a stinging article, "The Fatal Apostasy of the Modern Church." In it Lewis asked,

> But what does the modern church believe? The church is becoming creedless as rapidly as the innovators can have their way. The "Confession of Faith"—what is happening to it? Or what about the "new" confessions that one sees and hears—suitable enough, one imagines, for, say, a fraternal order. And as for the Apostles' Creed—"our people will not say it any more"; which means apparently that our people, having some difficulties over the Virgin Birth and the resurrection of the body, have elected the easy way of believing in nothing at all—certainly not in "the Holy Catholic Church."[1]

So for Methodists, the early quarter of this century was a time of serious theological transition.

While the liberalism of this era was never accepted by the grass roots of our Church, it was embraced by many leaders of our boards, publications, and institutions of higher education. It is this legacy, theologically, that has been passed on to subsequent generations of Methodists in this century.

THE BEGINNING OF GOOD NEWS

In this theological setting Good News was born. It began late in 1965 at a business lunch.

Chuck Keysor, recently graduated from Garrett Theological Seminary and pastoring in Elgin, Illinois, met for lunch with James Wall, editor of the Methodist ministers' magazine, *New Christian Advocate* (Wall is now editor of *Christian Century*).

During lunch the conversation turned toward the evangelical wing of the Methodist Church. Knowing this was Keysor's orientation, Wall asked Chuck, "Why don't you write an article for us describing the central beliefs and convictions of this part of our Church?"

The invitation led to the writing of "Methodism's Silent Minority," published in the July 14, 1966 issue of *New Christian Advocate*.

Chuck's article identified and expanded upon several of the major convictions shared by those who stand in the tradition of historic Christianity. Those theological convictions included:

1) a high view of the inspiration and reliability of Holy Scripture; 2) the virgin birth of Christ; 3) the substitutionary atonement of Christ; 4) the physical resurrection of Christ; and 5) the return of Christ.

In response to his article, to his amazement, Keysor received over two hundred letters and phone calls, mostly from Methodist pastors. Two themes surfaced in the responses: first, "I thought I was the only one left in our Church who believes these things," and second, "I feel so alone—so cut off from the leadership and organization of my Church!"

It was immediately clear that evangelicals were "out there" in Methodism. It was equally clear that they were suffering from isolation, discouragement, and lack of representation in leadership positions of the Church.

A number of those responding said, "Why can't our denomination have one magazine which publishes articles like this? Those of us who are conservative need a forum for our views. We feel excluded."

Keysor began to ponder those questions. Why, indeed, should the denomination which began with the evangelistic thrust of the Wesleys and Francis Asbury be without a voice for orthodoxy?

At the same time, Keysor knew well what it would take to launch a magazine. As a graduate of Medill School of Journalism, Northwestern University, Chuck had worked as managing editor of the *Kiwanis* Magazine, Methodism's *Together* magazine, and with the David C. Cook Publishing Company.

As he pondered and prayed over the letters and phone calls he had received, Chuck felt led to start a magazine which would be a "Forum for Scriptural Christianity" for "Methodism's Silent Minority."

So in March of 1967, the first issue of *Good News* was run off in a small print shop in Elgin. Young people from the Grace Methodist Church youth group helped assemble the sections and afix the six thousand three hundred labels that Chuck's wife, Marge, had previously typed. With a prayer, they delivered the loaded sacks to the Post Office and *Good News* was on its way.

Responses to the first issue were both varied and enthusiastic. A disgruntled Methodist in Auburn, Alabama, wrote, "Your magazine is JUNK!" But Carl F. H. Henry, then editor of the prestigious *Christianity Today,* wrote, "A mighty fine beginning—congratulations!"

As interest mounted, Chuck chose twelve persons to be the original directors of Good News. These directors assembled in Elgin for the first Good News Board meeting in May 1967.

Today the ministry of Good News is directed by an expanded board of forty United Methodists—pastors and laypersons from across America. All important policy decisions are made by this board and implemented by a staff of seventeen persons working with an annual budget of nearly $700,000. The national office in Wilmore, Kentucky, publishes the now bimonthly *Good News* magazine—in a new, full-sized, four-color format—for over twenty thousand United Methodist readers.

THE RENEWAL GROUP CONNECTION

Soon after Good News began, Methodists across the country began organizing regional renewal groups sympathetic with Good News. These groups function within many of the Church's seventy-four annual conferences (comparable to a diocese or presbytery).

Each annual conference meets yearly to conduct the business of the Church in its area. The state of Ohio, for example, has two separate annual conferences. But in the sparsely-populated Far West, several states may make up just one.

Over the years, these annual conference evangelical renewal groups have become the grass-roots network for the Good News movement. Today probably 65 percent of our annual conferences have some kind of renewal fellowship.

These groups represent a cluster of like-minded evangelicals who have felt a need to meet for fellowship, encouragement, prayer, and for mapping strategies to broaden the influence of evangelicalism within their annual conferences.

The program and structure of these groups vary according to their needs. Good News has never attempted to charter any of the local groups. Rather, we have tried to serve them by providing guidance and resources for their renewal ministries.

The renewal group in my annual conference is a good example. The East Ohio Evangelical Fellowship (EOEF), started in 1969, has spawned a number of ministries which have become a vital part of the conference's continuing program.

Our first effort was a senior high summer camp experience called Senior High Youth Festival. Planned with a definite evangelical flavor, the youth experience soon became the largest senior high youth camp in the annual conference. Soon a Junior High Festival was launched and later a similar experience for fifth- and sixth-grade youth.

In a few years, the EOEF started a Youth Witness Tour for high school youth. It quickly grew to involve some one hundred and fifty youth touring Ohio in three musical ensembles each summer. The young people spend an intensive two weeks during the summer sharing their faith through music and spoken word all across the conference.

Many high school youth have found Christ as Savior through all these EOEF-sponsored youth experiences. After the first few years, born-again, dedicated Christian youth from these various programs began to move into places of leadership on the Conference Council on Youth Ministries. The entire conference youth program felt the impact of these ministries.

The renewal group in East Ohio has also sponsored retreats, seminars, training sessions for general conference, dialogues with the bishop and district superintendents, a regular newsletter in which evangelicals speak to issues before the Church, and a large dinner during our annual conference week. This banquet, which draws together some three hundred to four hundred evangelicals for an evening of inspiration and encouragement, is the highlight of annual conference for many of us.

When renewal groups were first being formed, some Church leaders were critical. They predicted renewal groups would be divisive. However, I believe these groups have actually been a healing factor for our Church.

Why? Because for years Methodist evangelicals had felt like second-class citizens in their Church. They had been ignored and overlooked for places of leadership in our Church. So, for the sake of survival, many pastors had simply tuned out the Church's national program, deciding just to work hard for a fruitful ministry in their local churches.

But that can be dangerous. Pastors can become isolated

and bitter that way. When this happens, spiritual defeat is not far away.

So, for clergy struggling to be faithful in a liberal denomination, regional renewal groups have been and remain a source of much needed fellowship and support. They have been a means of healing, not division.

CONVOCATIONS FEED THE FLOCK

By the third annual meeting of the Good News Board in 1969, people in conference renewal groups had begun urging Good News to sponsor a national meeting. The challenge seemed overwhelming. How could an unofficial group with little national recognition and no Church funding hold a national convocation?

But the directors prayed about it, asking Texas pastor Mike Walker to explore the possibilities. The result once again proved that God was at work in the young movement. The Convocation of United Methodists for Evangelical Christianity was held in August 1970 at the Adolphus Hotel in Dallas, Texas. To the amazement of the Good News leadership, over sixteen hundred United Methodists came—from all across the country!

The Holy Spirit drew the group together in a remarkable way. Lives were changed by the power of Christ. Discouraged United Methodists were empowered anew for service. All who came shared in an unforgettable experience of love and unity which remains to this day one of the mountaintop experiences of Good News.

At the Dallas Convocation, United Methodists received new hope for the future of their Church. They dared to dream of a new day of revival, renewal, and faithfulness to the Biblical message.

Every summer since 1970, Good News has sponsored national convocations. And every summer hundreds have gathered. From Dallas to Dover, Delaware; from Cincinnati to Fayetteville, Arkansas; from Ashland, Ohio to Colorado Springs, they have come for fellowship, inspiration, and instruction.

Convocations have provided Good News with a national platform for addressing some of the major issues facing our

Church. But for the most part, the convocations serve to encourage and enable lonely and dejected United Methodists who are willing to travel great distances to find fellowship with like-minded United Methodists.

As I have visited with our Good News pastors over the past five years, I have realized how many of them are using programs they learned about at a Good News convo. Whether it's Marriage Enrichment, Trinity Bible Studies, or the Faith Promise Support for second-mile missions giving, pastors often say, "I learned about this program in a seminar at a Good News convo."

For many, a national convocation has provided the encouragement needed to remain United Methodists. In Colorado Springs in 1986, a couple walked up to me and said, "You know, Jim, when we came here we were so discouraged, we were planning to leave the Church. But our hearts have been renewed, and we're going back to our church with new hope now." Such testimonies are not unusual from convo-goers.

THE FIGHT OVER CHURCH SCHOOL LITERATURE

One of the earliest concerns raised by Good News was the poor quality of the denomination's church school literature.

Sunday school materials frequently lacked a strong, Biblical base and often departed from the historic Methodist doctrines. For many years evangelicals had been frustrated but had no way to address the problem.

What was wrong with the material? In 1968 *Good News* carried a three-part article evaluating Methodism's new adult curriculum. One reviewer summed it up this way:

> What is missing here, for the believer, is a particular and sustained Biblical theology. We find many Bible verses and references to Bible stories, but no theology per se. . . .
> This reviewer looked in vain for any word about salvation, any good news about the atonement of Jesus Christ, or any hint about the possibility of spiritual new birth through the shed blood of our Lord and Savior. . . .

This evaluation was the first effort at a unified evangelical objection to weak, non-Biblical denominational curriculum. It helped many other Methodist evangelicals realize that others shared their dissatisfaction with the Church's curriculum. Thus, Good News helped expose the seriousness of the curriculum problem for the first time nationally.

The next year, 1969, Good News leaders met for the first time to dialogue with the Church's curriculum editors and officials. Good News leaders shared their frustration over the Church's weak, un-Biblical curriculum. Denominational leaders responded in a way that seemed arrogant and condescending. One bishop generalized to the Good News delegation that *all* scholars support the Bultmannian view that much of the Bible is "myth," and that whether Jesus really lived or not isn't important.

But at least the dialogue had begun, and more such sessions followed. And increasingly the leadership of the Publishing House in Nashville began to realize they exist to serve the whole Church.

By 1974, Good News began hearing from pastors who were dissatisfied with the Church's confirmation materials for youth. After surveying some twelve hundred United Methodist pastors, Good News was convinced of the critical need in local churches for some kind of new, Biblically-sound confirmation literature.

So, in 1975 Good News published its new *We Believe* confirmation series for junior high youth. United Methodist pastors received it enthusiastically. The new resource was thoroughly Wesleyan, faithful to the denomination's membership vows, and focused clearly on bringing young persons to commitment to Christ. *We Believe* has gone through eleven printings since 1975. In 1979, a senior high/adult adaptation was published which remains in use today.

A 1985 Good News evaluation of denominational curriculum revealed significant improvement in our church school literature. Our curriculum editors are increasingly concerned about producing materials acceptable to evangelicals. They are also seeking and using evangelicals to write more curriculum.

Though our denominational curriculum is much improved, it still is not yet consistently reliable. But Good News leaders agree it has come a long way. Many Church leaders credit Good News with bringing about the needed dialogue and feedback that produced the change.

Good News continues to monitor church school literature, evaluating both doctrinal content and the possible introduction of new God-language which would be unacceptable to most United Methodist evangelicals.

In early 1987, the United Methodist Publishing House announced a brand-new, major Bible-study program. Fashioned after the highly successful Bethel Bible Study and Trinity Bible Studies, the new unit was welcomed enthusiastically by evangelicals.

THE STRUGGLE AGAINST DOCTRINAL COMPROMISE

Good News has always believed that lasting renewal will not come to the denomination until there is a renewal of our historic evangelical theology. We also believe doctrinal compromise and unbelief have been at the heart of United Methodism's tragic decline.

And it was this theological confusion and outright unfaithfulness that characterized Methodism in the mid-1960s when Good News was launched. During those years, Methodism was well-organized, always striving to be "relevant." But we were sadly anemic in spiritual power. This was the era in which the Church was "letting the world set the agenda." All the while, the Biblical agenda was languishing from neglect.

So from the beginning, Good News has sought to be a clear voice for the evangelical faith within Methodism. This concern is at the heart of all that we do.

But what do we mean by *evangelical?* This question is important, for in recent years it has become increasingly popular to be an "evangelical." But many of us fear this popularity is more cosmetic than substantive. The term *evangelical* is rich in doctrinal content. When we speak of the evangelical faith, we must be sure of what we mean.

One helpful definition that describes who the evangelical is comes from Carl F. H. Henry, the dean of evangelical theologians in America. Henry says,

Evangelical Christians are thus marked by their devotion to the sure Word of the Bible; they are committed to the inspired Scriptures as the divine rule of faith and practice. They affirm the fundamental doctrines of the Gospel, including the incarnation and the virgin birth of Christ,

His sinless life, substitutionary atonement, and bodily resurrection as the ground of God's forgiveness of sinners,
justification by faith alone, and the spiritual regeneration
of all who trust in the redemptive work of Jesus Christ.[2]

So for Good News as well as other evangelicals, being an
evangelical has always implied adherence to certain doctrinal
tenets.

As an expression of concern for this evangelical faith, the
Good News Board authorized a Theology and Doctrine Task
Force in 1974. Chaired by Dr. Paul A. Mickey, associate professor of pastoral theology at Duke University's Divinity School,
the task force's goal was to prepare a clear, fresh statement of
"Scriptural Christianity." The statement was to be faithful to
both the Methodist and the Evangelical United Brethren traditions. (The Methodists and EUBs merged in 1968 to form the
present United Methodist Church.)

After eighteen months work, the task force presented a
statement to the Good News Board which was formally adopted on July 20, 1975, at the Lake Junaluska Assembly. The
Junaluska Affirmation, as it was called, was a brief, systematic
summary—a fresh restatement—of the essentials of "Scriptural
Christianity" in the Wesleyan tradition.

The Junaluska Affirmation contains a brief preamble, then
sections on the Holy Trinity, God the Father, God the Son, God
the Holy Spirit, Humanity, The Holy Scriptures, Salvation, The
Church, and Ethics. It may well be the first new systematic
Methodist statement of faith-essentials since Methodism came
to America in the 1700s.

In 1980, as a sequel to the new statement, Zondervan
published Dr. Paul Mickey's commentary on the Junaluska
Affirmation, a book entitled *Essentials of Wesleyan Theology.* It
provides verse by verse commentary on the Junaluska Affirmation and remains an important work for pastors and laypeople
interested in Methodist doctrine. Before persons are elected to
the Good News board, they must attest to basic agreement
with the content of the Junaluska Affirmation.

At the 1972 General Conference, a new guiding principle
for theological formulation—called theological pluralism—was
adopted along with a whole new doctrinal statement for United
Methodists.

The tenet of theological pluralism, though never defined, was an attempt to be open to the wide variety of theological views found within Methodism. However, the effect of pluralism was to diminish serious theological reflection in the Church. For instead of helping clarify Methodism's doctrinal malaise, it only added further confusion. The reason is that theological pluralism has helped legitimize erroneous doctrine by giving validity to all competing views, no matter how contradictory they might be.

For example, when a young pastor challenged a United Methodist seminary professor for denying the bodily resurrection of Christ, his district superintendent reproved him, saying, "Ed, you must remember that you are in a Church that embraces theological pluralism."

Another illustration of our theological plight was seen several years ago in *Christian Century*'s "How My Mind Has Changed" series. Four persons associated with United Methodist seminaries were included in the series.

From these four professors we learn that:

1. Critical analysis of the Bible has rendered unacceptable the traditional Protestant principle of Scripture as norm.

2. One professor has little time for inherited theology.

3. Another rejects all absolutist views of Biblical religion. The triumphalistic presumptions about the superiority of Yahwism to Ba'alism, Christianity to paganism were no longer possible.

4. The idea of salvation only in Christ "has become unacceptable to all except a minority of dogmatic diehards."

5. The "Eternal One" is Allah of Islam, Krishna of Hinduism, Nirvana of Buddhism, as well as the Father of Jesus Christ.

And on it goes.

Fortunately, the 1984 General Conference realized the Church's dire predicament. It authorized a task force to prepare and present a new doctrinal statement for approval at our 1986 General Conference. Many feel this action was the result of Good News' persistent efforts at doctrinal reform over the past ten years.

Good News also addressed the theological crisis by publishing a book in 1986 entitled, *Basic United Methodist Beliefs: An Evangelical View.* The volume is a collection of articles on basic doctrine by thirteen different United Methodist leaders. Written in a style appropriate for church study groups, the entire first printing sold out in five months. This was further evidence that United Methodists are longing for a clear statement of Wesleyan doctrine.

In the fall of 1986, Good News published *The Problem of Pluralism: Recovering United Methodist Identity.* This scholarly work by Jerry L. Walls is the most thorough, if not the only, evangelical critique of theological pluralism available for United Methodists today.

So from the beginning Good News has sought to restore the power and influence of historic Christianity within the Church by helping it recover its evangelical, Wesleyan faith.

EFFORTS AT REFORM IN THEOLOGICAL SEMINARIES

With its basic concerns being theological, Good News has had long-standing problems with United Methodism's thirteen theological seminaries, all of which have been dominated by liberal theology.

Students attending our seminaries have often encountered opposition and even hostility toward their evangelical beliefs. Many have admitted they just kept quiet and said little during their seminary days. They felt this was necessary to survive in the liberal theological environment. Some have claimed, with supportive evidence, that their grades suffered because of their evangelical views. For certain, our seminaries have been the most unpluralistic institutions in our Church.

In 1975, United Methodist evangelist Dr. Edmund W. Robb, Jr. criticized United Methodist theological education in a blistering address at our national convocation. Institutional leaders fumed and fussed about the message, which received national coverage.

However, Robb's hard-hitting message led to a new friendship with Dr. Albert C. Outler, United Methodism's premier Wesleyan scholar. And out of this friendship came the formation of a new organization called A Fund for Theological Education (AFTE).

The purpose of AFTE is to help fund competent young evangelical scholars in their Ph.D. programs with an understanding that these young scholars will teach in United Methodist colleges and seminaries. To date, over forty-five John Wesley Fellows, as they are called, have participated in the program, with five new fellows accepted each year.

While AFTE is not a Good News program, it has drawn strong and enthusiastic support from the Good News constituency.

Some see the AFTE program as one of the most visionary and hopeful strategies for the recovery of evangelicalism within the Church. The AFTE board has included such noted United Methodist leaders as Dr. Outler, Bishops Earl Hunt and Finis Crutchfield, Dr. Kenneth Kinghorn, Dr. Paul Morell, and Dr. R. L. Kirk. Already, gifted young AFTE fellows are being named to faculties of our denominational seminaries.

Good News has also tried to encourage evangelical seminarians through a newsletter, *Catalyst*. Published four times during each academic year, *Catalyst* provides scholarly evangelical resources for United Methodist seminarians. For eleven years it has been sent free to over five thousand United Methodist seminarians all across the country.

From its inception, *Catalyst* was edited by Rev. Mike Walker, presently pastor of the thirty-two hundred-member Tyler Street United Methodist Church in Dallas, Texas. After steering it faithfully for those eleven years, in 1986 Walker turned over the editor's job to Dr. Joel Green, an AFTE John Wesley Fellow and currently dean of New College, Berkley.

As a further effort to see reform in our denominational seminaries, Good News initiated a program in 1977 which sent teams of United Methodist evangelicals to visit all of our Church-related seminaries. Teams were welcomed at eleven of our thirteen seminaries. During the one- and two-day visits, team members engaged in dialogue with faculty, administration, and students in an effort to articulate the concerns of evangelicals. Always, our plea was for the seminary to enlist more faculty members who are clearly evangelical and that persons invited as lecturers and chapel speakers include clearly-identified evangelicals.

For some of our seminaries, the visitation program resulted in a continuing dialogue over the next few years. And while the dominant theological commitment of our denominational seminaries is still quite liberal, some are beginning to invite evangelicals to join their faculties. And with the growing impact of the AFTE program, we believe that the future of United Methodist theological education belongs to evangelicalism.

THE CONTROVERSY WITH UNITED METHODISM'S MISSIONS PROGRAM

In 1973, Good News turned its focus to United Methodism's program of world missions. Dr. David Seamands, Good News board member and former missionary to India, told a national convocation audience that United Methodists were deeply concerned about the Church's shrinking missionary force.

Seamands also noted that evangelicals were concerned about the lopsidedness of United Methodism's official missions board, the General Board of Global Ministries (GBGM). He charged that board staff seemed mainly concerned about social reform. They showed little concern for matters of faith, eternity, conversion, or establishing new churches.

Discontent grew until 1974 when seventy-two United Methodist evangelicals from twenty-three states gathered in Dallas, Texas, for a Churchwide consortium to discuss the direction and nature of the Church's world missions program. Those gathered voted to establish an independent Evangelical Missions Council (EMC). They also authorized their newly-formed executive committee to dialogue with GBGM leaders to establish "a clear and trustworthy channel for evangelical missions *within* the church's mission board."

However, the results of these early dialogues proved disappointing. Seamands, who had been elected first chairman of EMC, recalled about those early discussions, "We learned that the unfortunate gulf separating us from the GBGM policy-makers was wide and deep."

In 1976, the EMC ministry entered a new phase. It became a task force of Good News. And rather than just dialoguing with denominational leaders, EMC decided to work to get local churches to come alive with a passion for worldwide missions.

To put wheels under the vision of ministry to local churches, Good News hired Rev. Virgil Maybray as full-time executive secretary of EMC. Virgil, an experienced mission-minded pastor from the Western Pennsylvania Conference, spent most of his time speaking and consulting with local churches about expanding their missions programs, especially through second-mile, faith-promise giving.

During eight years with Good News' EMC, Virgil worked in over three hundred and fifty United Methodist churches in some thirty-five states and saw several millions of dollars raised for the cause of missions. At least $1 million was channeled through GBGM's Advance Special Program to support official United Methodist programs and personnel.

Between 1976 and 1983, EMC leaders continued to dialogue with GBGM leaders, but the situation had only gotten worse. The total number of United Methodist missionaries serving full-time overseas had declined to under five hundred from a high of over fifteen hundred just twenty years earlier. It began to look like we were headed out of the missionary-sending business. Liberation theology clearly had become the controlling theology of the United Methodist missions agency.

And so, despite no less than twenty-four dialogue sessions between EMC and GBGM leaders over the previous decade, by 1983 Good News and EMC leaders had concluded that further conversations were useless. It was time for Good News to form a supplemental mission sending agency, though we knew such an action would be highly controversial.

But before the Good News plans were made public, a larger movement began. It was sparked by the election of Peggy Billings as the new head of GBGM's overseas missions program. Billings was the most radical and controversial of the candidates being considered for the post.

Only a few weeks after Billings was elected, a group of twenty-nine large-church pastors and four missions professors met in St. Louis in November of 1983. After intense discussion and much prayer, the group decided they would form a new "supplemental" missions agency. It would be called The Mission Society for United Methodists.

The word "supplemental" is important, as the founders of the new body insisted that support for it should come from second-mile missions giving in local United Methodist churches. They were not competing for the apportionment dollars that support the denomination's official mission board.

The new Mission Society had a larger constituency than Good News because some who came to the St. Louis meeting had not previously related to the evangelical caucus.

Dr. L. D. Thomas, pastor of First United Methodist Church in Tulsa, and Dr. Ira Galloway, pastor of First United Methodist Church in Peoria, gave strategic leadership in the formative days of the new society. The group's board named Rev. H. T. Maclin to be its chief executive. Maclin, a former missionary to Africa under GBGM, was serving as southeastern jurisdiction field representative for GBGM when he joined the new society.

When the new missions body was announced, Good News decided to phase out its EMC ministry and merge its resources with the new organization. Virgil Maybray, for eight years the EMC top executive, was hired as the number two executive with the Mission Society.

Since its founding in 1983, the Mission Society has moved with amazing speed to get persons to the mission field. Sixteen persons are already serving on the field. Over five hundred persons have inquired about service, and over one hundred and sixty have made application.

The Mission Society for United Methodists is an independent sending body. It has no official relationship with Good News. However, our constituencies obviously overlap. And nearly everyone involved with Good News is enthused about and supportive of the new society and its clearly evangelical agenda, which is to respond to Christ's call to ". . . go and make disciples of all nations."

Though the new supplemental agency has been bitterly opposed by the leadership of the denomination's official mission board, The Mission Society for United Methodists continues to establish both its own credibility and an impressive track record. It will survive the opposition from the Church's liberals. It will outlive its harshest critics. It is here to stay.

Meanwhile, Good News will continue to press GBGM, with its massive staff and over $90 million budget, to be faithful to its Biblical mandate to evangelize the world.

REFORM THROUGH THE CHURCH'S POLITICAL PROCESS

Attempts to bring reform through the Church's legislative process have played a major role in the story of Good News.

As evangelicals began to organize, they had to decide how they would relate to the Church's nonevangelical climate. They could act as if nothing were wrong. They could passively submit to things that violated their faith and conscience. They could go find a different Church. They could ignore Church policies and focus on building a spiritually vital subchurch within the denomination. Or they could try to channel their influence for positive change.

Good News chose the latter, deciding to get involved in the denomination's decision-making process.

The 1972 General Conference in Atlanta was Good News' first effort to be involved in the legislative process. We prepared and distributed ten petitions and four resolutions, urging evangelicals across the Church to send them in individually or from their local churches.

What was the Good News agenda in this first major political effort? The petitions were asking the Church to limit the tenure of Church executives, allow laypeople to vote on the ordination of clergy, use Church funds only for purposes solicited, give local churches greater representation in curriculum development, allow freedom for churches to designate money given, withdraw from COCU deliberations, and make Christ's Lordship the denomination's top priority.

Good News also, for the first time, maintained an organized evangelical presence at General Conference. Board members Bob Sprinkle and Helen Rhea Coppedge (present Good News board chairperson) cranked out occasional newsletters giving the Good News perspective on issues. They also made contacts with sympathetic delegates seeking to establish evangelical consensus on some of the issues.

But for evangelicals, the 1972 General Conference was a disaster. It approved of abortion. The homosexual issue surfaced with some strength. The gargantuan General Board of Global Ministries was born. And delegates accepted a new doctrinal statement which made "theological pluralism" official.

By the 1976 General Conference in Portland, Good News was better organized. A team of twenty-five workers were on hand to observe the ten legislative committees, follow the strategy in the plenary sessions, and lobby for evangelical concerns. This effort marked the first time ever that evangelicals had been an organized presence at a general conference.

At Portland, the push to accept homosexuality exploded in

full force. The United Methodist Council on Youth Ministries openly supported homosexual ordination. And a homosexual caucus was formed to lobby for "gay" rights before and during the 1976 General Conference. The leader of the homosexual caucus was even invited to speak for the homosexual cause before one of the conference's legislative committees.

But the Good News team worked to counter this push. Robert Snyder, seasoned pastor from the East Ohio Conference, joined Sprinkle and Coppedge in providing leadership to the Portland team.

And when the smoke had cleared, the delegates had rejected prohomosexual efforts to remove the key Social Principles statement: ". . . we do not condone the practice of homosexuality. . . ."

Without a doubt, the Good News presence in Portland had been strategic in defeating the homosexual network's push to make the practice of homosexuality an alternate Christian lifestyle.

The pattern set in Portland was expanded for the 1980 General Conference. Virginia Law Shell, Good News board member, and her husband, Don, took responsibility for heading the Good News effort. And with a budget of over $60,000, it was the largest and best organized yet.

Virginia, widely known as a former missionary to the Congo and cofounder of the Board of Discipleship's Marriage Enrichment Program, gave strong leadership to a Good News team of sixty-five in Indianapolis. Virginia's husband, Don, a corporate computer executive, brought unusual skills and wisdom to the leadership team.

George and Eva Wicks, from Dayton, Indiana, coordinated a nationwide prayer chain involving over fifty thousand United Methodists who undergirded the 1980 effort at Indianapolis.

Good News dispatched teams of trained observers to track the course of events in the ten legislative committees. We also sponsored breakfasts for delegates, using the time to prepare for the day's issues and strategies.

Good News prepared and sent out over fourteen thousand petition packets with detailed instructions on writing petitions and with model petitions on seventeen topics. Issues included designated giving, abortion, homosexuality, the family, and strengthening the Church's theological statement.

A new innovation in 1980 was a series of four carefully written letters sent in advance to all General Conference delegates. These letters gave the rationale for the stand Good News was taking on various issues. While not all delegates agreed with our views, they expressed appreciation for receiving an early and clear articulation of them.

A major breakthrough of the 1980 General Conference came as a result of the efforts of a then little-known layman, David Jessup. Having become concerned about Church dollars going to radical leftist causes, Jessup authored a petition on board and agency accountability. He also followed it through the legislative process. The result was that General Conference passed the new legislation which required each general agency to report cash grants given to "organizations, individuals, coalitions, consultations, programs and entities not formally part of the church."

In addition, Jessup's efforts and his association with Ed Robb led to Robb's founding of the Institute for Religion and Democracy (IRD). The agenda of the IRD is to bring a renewed concern for religious liberty, democratic values, and human rights to the international affairs program of the mainline churches in America. Since then, United Methodists for Religious Liberty and Human Rights, a denominational branch of the IRD, has been organized.

Evangelicals won few other victories at Indianapolis in 1980, although the Church reaffirmed its Biblical stand on the homosexual issue. What the Good News effort did gain was credibility and respect. Many delegates and Church leaders expressed appreciation for the professional and gracious nature of the Good News presence.

That in turn laid a good foundation for a similar major Good News effort at the 1984 General Conference in Baltimore. Again led by Virginia and Don Shell, the same strategies were employed. Petitions were prepared and sent out. Position papers were mailed to all delegates. An on-site team of some twenty-seven persons again monitored legislative committees and followed floor strategy.

But 1984 was different. Of the twelve Good News petitions, seven of them were passed in one form or another. Delegates, both young and old, spoke of a different spirit at Baltimore from previous General Conferences. A bishop re-

marked that in twenty-six years of attending General Conferences, he could not remember sensing as much emphasis on
prayer and spiritual concerns.

Again, the Good News effort had been low-key. Following
one important vote, a Church leader approached Virginia Shell
and said, "Virginia, I've been wondering just where Good
News has been the past few days. But when that last vote was
taken and they announced the results, then I knew."

The Baltimore General Conference took a number of actions that evangelicals applauded. Most significant was legislation banning the ordination and appointment of self-avowed,
practicing homosexuals. This was a major victory for the evangelical forces. It also authorized a task force to prepare a new
doctrinal statement for the Church by 1988. Further, it authorized a commission to study the mission of the Church. While
celebrating the two hundredth anniversary of the founding of
Methodism in America, the Baltimore General Conference was
willing to acknowledge that United Methodism was danger-
ously unsure of its doctrinal moorings and its mission.

This General Conference also expressed deep dissatisfaction with the policies of the General Board of Global Ministries. Negative attitudes surfaced frequently both in the hall-
ways as well as on the floor of the conference. And while the
bishops perfunctorily affirmed GBGM as the sole sending agency for the Church (a mild slap at the newly-formed Mission
Society), they exhorted GBGM at length to get its act together
and not neglect its mandate to evangelize.

Have the time, money, and energy spent in the legislative
process been worth it? We believe so. Not always for great
victories gained. But for some. And also for helping check the
Church's drift in radical directions. We have raised the visibility
of evangelical concerns. We have spoken to Church programs
from the platform of Biblical principles. We have demonstrated
a dogged desire to remain a part of the Church—which has for
so long ignored and manipulated evangelicals—and have shown
we are willing to work for change within the system.

For sure, Good News' active presence at our General Conferences has become a source of great hope for discouraged
evangelicals. They now know there is an organized effort for
reform and renewal in the Church they love and are struggling
to stay in.

REFLECTIONS ON THE STRUGGLE FOR RENEWAL

In 1981, I assumed responsibilities as editor/executive secretary of Good News. Our founding editor and chief executive for fifteen years had decided to step down. Chuck was a giant in the eyes of many of us. And he was a personal friend.

By 1983, Chuck felt he must sever his relationship with the United Methodist Church. That year he transferred his credentials to the Evangelical Covenant Church of North America. In October of 1985, Chuck died from a recurrence of cancer while pastoring in Clearwater, Florida.

The struggle for renewal which Chuck helped launch is formidable and often unpleasant. Many United Methodists would rather not know about their Church's problems. They would rather not hear about 1.8 million members lost in the last two decades, or about the decimation of our church schools, which lost 2.1 million members during the same period, or about the push for the acceptance of homosexuality.

And this is understandable. People want to believe in their Church and the rightness of what it is doing.

But the problems persist. As this is written, a known homosexual continues under appointment as a United Methodist minister. The push by feminists to change the way we address God continues. "God our Father and Mother" is heard with increasing frequency in public services. And our official missions agency continues unabashed in its commitment to liberation theology.

So until the Church is aware of the gravity of its problems, we will not see prayerful concern for renewal. We will see only satisfaction with the *status quo*.

One of the greatest encouragements to evangelicals recently has been the courageous leadership of one of our newly-elected bishops, Richard B. Wilke.

In a book that has shaken the denomination, Wilke says, "Our sickness is more serious than we at first suspected. We are in trouble, you and I, and our United Methodist Church. . . . Once we were a Wesleyan revival, full of enthusiasm, fired by the Spirit. . . . Now we are tired, listless, fueled only by the nostalgia of former days."[3]

Denominational leaders are beginning to address our spiritual sickness. And while some evangelicals have lost hope for revival in the Church, others of us believe that the winds of renewal are already blowing. But we are also aware that this great transformation for which we pray will not come as a result of human strategies but as a result of the power of God. We believe that "with God all things are possible."

A few years ago, a new fellowship called United Methodists Renewal, Services, Fellowship was formed as a renewal effort for those United Methodists who are a part of the charismatic movement. Though avoiding involvement in Church issues, this renewal effort is also earnestly seeking the Holy Spirit's fresh anointing upon our once-great Church. It reminds us that God is at work on a number of fronts.

For those involved in this kind of struggle, let me make several observations.

First, the ministry of renewal in ours and other mainline Churches must employ a long-term strategy. We did not get into this spiritual and theological decline overnight. It is the result of years of unfaithfulness. And in this age of the instantaneous, our patience can easily be depleted.

Also, those involved in the struggle must be careful not to succumb to bitterness or cynicism. As the war is waged, unfortunately you learn more about the Church than you ever wanted to know. Sometimes leaders vindictively resist evangelical overtures for change.

Third, the need within United Methodism is not for more evangelical pastors, though we would welcome that. The need is for evangelicals already among us to stop being intimidated by a liberal leadership or compromised by their own aspirations for advancement. It's time we lifted our voices boldly on behalf of the evangelical faith.

That also means, then, that evangelicals must abandon the luxury of sitting on the sidelines criticizing while others play the game. We need to be willing to get involved at every level of the Church. This is especially difficult for evangelicals, for they tend to find personal satisfaction in local church ministry. This is not always the case with liberal clergy. They often find their satisfaction working in conference structures. This is not surprising either, for the liberal agenda is generally not well received by grass-roots United Methodists.

Fifth, pastors must realize their responsibility as leaders to address their Church's critical problems. To do so can be an expression of one's love for the Church. In fact, when ordained, United Methodist ministers promise to "defend the Church against all doctrine contrary to God's Word." That task is not always pleasant, but it must be done.

Finally, evangelicals must join to end the politicizing of the Church. For far too many United Methodists, the Church has become an arena for their political agenda. They have little time for proclamation, evangelism, or spiritual formation. What makes them salivate is speaking to *issues*, for that is really "where the action is." Or so they believe.

For sure, Christians must be involved in the moral and ethical issues of the day. But the Church must avoid partisan politics. This is always destructive for the Church.

Evangelicals must insist that to use the Church to advance one's partisan political agenda is to exploit the Church. Members and others come to church to worship and hear the Word of God read and preached. They do not come to be doused with political opinion.

The mandate, then, for evangelicals within United Methodism and other mainline Churches is to be a faithful voice for the New Testament faith. Under the anointing of the Holy Spirit, we must contend for the faith but without becoming contentious in our spirits.

Or, in the words of Paul to young Timothy, our task is to "guard the good deposit" which has been entrusted to us, all the while praying that God will do what we cannot—that is, bring vital, lasting renewal to His Church.

A DIRECTORY OF RENEWAL GROUPS IN THE UNITED METHODIST CHURCH

Good News—A Forum for Scriptural Christianity
308 East Main Street
Wilmore, Kentucky 40390
606/858-4661

The Mission Society for United Methodists
246 Sycamore Street
Box 1103
Decatur, Georgia 30030
404/378-8746

A Foundation for Theological Education (AFTE)
P.O. Box 1542
Marshall, Texas 75671
214/938-8305

United Methodists for Religious Liberty and Human Rights
729 15th Street, N.W., Suite 900
Washington, D.C. 20005
202/393-3200

United Methodist Renewal Services Fellowship
P.O. Box 50086
Nashville, Tennessee 37205-0086
615/327-2700

THE REV. JOHN R. THROOP

is associate rector of Christ Episcopal Church, Shaker Heights, Ohio. He is also coordinator for several national Episcopalian renewal conferences. Rev. Throop holds degrees from the University of Chicago (B.A. in history) and the School of Theology of the University of the South (M.Div.). He has contributed articles to such journals as *Christianity Today, Leadership, His, The Living Church, New Oxford Review,* and *Christian Century.* His first book, *Shape Up from the Inside Out,* appeared in 1986.

T W O
The Episcopal Church
John R. Throop

T he great evangelist Billy Sunday was once said to have remarked that the Episcopal Church is a "sleeping giant." Some would say that, from the standpoint of renewal among mainline Protestant denominations, the Episcopal Church has been nearly comatose. The denomination has been visible and active and at times controversial during the last twenty years; but it has neither experienced widespread spiritual renewal nor significant numerical growth. The Episcopal Church is at a turning-point in its history. Only authentic, deep, purging renewal will enable the denomination to provide essential leadership in America as we move into the next century.

The official leadership of the denomination appears to stress renewal; one can even find publications and seminars that talk about the need for renewal. Unfortunately, the word *renewal* in its Episcopalian contexts is a very vague word that is often used to refer to nothing more than any call for change, be it liturgical, social, institutional, or theological. In a denomination that has known so much turmoil and decline over the last twenty years, anything that seems to be good or that will produce good feelings tends to be called renewal.

When we examine *evangelical* renewal in the Episcopal Church, then, we must be very specific about what we mean; we must define the term. Such concern about giving the term a precise meaning means we risk becoming exclusive, an abhorrent notion to a denomination whose leaders stress inclusiveness with respect to every conceivable viewpoint. Genuine renewal, however, should not be confused with whatever Episcopalians happen to be doing at the moment; it is not to be identified with anything good that may happen to be taking place in the life of the Church. Renewal is something specific and wonderful, and, thank God, beyond human tinkering. It results from God's working in the Church and often occurs in spite of the people in that Church.

Fuzzy thinking about renewal in the Episcopal Church reflects a feature of the Anglican character. The Episcopal Church is part of the Anglican communion, that worldwide body of Churches which trace their origins to the Church of England. There are nearly seventy million Anglicans in twenty-seven self-governing Churches divided into four hundred and thirty dioceses in one hundred sixty-four countries. By far the largest number of Anglicans may be found in former British colonies in Africa and Asia. The Church of England is a state Church, supported by the English government. Hence, the Anglican Church was established wherever England ruled. These Churches, now on their own, still consider the Anglican tradition their way of being the Church in the world.

The Episcopal Church severed all formal ties with the Church of England during the Revolutionary War. It would have been a traitorous act to do otherwise in the newly independent United States. Nevertheless, the Episcopal Church retained the form of government and the order of ministry of the Church of England, as well as a similar *Book of Common Prayer*, the printed form of worship in Anglican churches. Legally, then, the Episcopal Church became independent of the Church of England; but theologically, spiritually, morally, and historically it has retained close ties. Those ties, particularly the history and tradition, or the "feel" of the Church, remain strong today. The Church of England remains the spiritual home of Episcopalians.

So the direction of the Episcopal Church, and the form and shape of renewal in it, reflect Anglican tradition and ethos. The Church of England is a Reformed Church—but very dissimilar to the continental Reformed Churches or the Church of Scotland (the Presbyterian Church) which trace their roots to the theological and spiritual leadership of Luther, Calvin, and Zwingli. We would hardly call Henry VIII a Reformer. In fact, he was an ardent foe of Luther. Henry was a rather good theologian himself, defending the Catholic Church in his anti-Lutheran tract, *The Defense of the Seven Sacraments* (1521). For this effort, Pope Leo X gave him the title "Defender of the

Faith." But Leo's successor, Clement VII, would not grant the divorce Henry eagerly wanted from Catherine of Aragon due to her inability to produce a male heir for the strong-willed king. It was over Clement's refusal to grant a divorce, rather than any significant doctrinal or theological difference, that Henry broke from Rome. Now there was an inherent English distaste for any outside rule, and the Church of England's relationship with Rome had frequently been quite stormy. There was much sympathy for Henry's action. Even so, if Henry had sired a son by Catherine, English church history might well have been different.

The origin and impetus of reform, then, were much different in England than on the continent, a fact which still influences the Anglican approach to faith today. The Reformation on the continent did influence the faith of the Church of England. For example, Thomas Cranmer, architect of the *Prayer Book,* was deeply influenced by Luther's writings. Henry relied upon Cranmer heavily for theological and liturgical direction in the Church of England as it grew further from Rome.

But the continental Reformation simply did not take theological root at this point in the English Church, influenced as it was by political factors. Henry was succeeded by his sickly son Edward VI, a young boy guided by Protestant advisors. He ruled, if one can call it that, from 1547 until his death in 1552. He was succeeded by his Roman Catholic sister Mary, who ruled from 1553-58. During her reign, she attempted to reinstitute her faith as the faith of the Church of England. She was popularly known as "Bloody Mary" because of the many Protestants who were put to death during her reign. When she died in 1558, she was succeeded by her sister Elizabeth I, who ruled from 1558 to 1603.

Elizabeth sympathized with the Protestants and steered the nation on a moderate religious course during her lengthy reign. She pressed for uniformity of faith, accepting neither Catholics nor Puritans in her middle way. She was also mindful of the conservative nature of her people. This middle way included all of the people in the realm in a state Church. The theological and spiritual direction of the Church of England *had* to be moderate if the people were to be united religiously.

From this brief historical overview, two points are relevant to understanding renewal in the Anglican tradition. First, the Reformation, as experienced in England, was not driven by theological principle but by political expediency. Secondly, when the Reformation finally did take root during Elizabeth's reign, the Church of England was characterized by reasonableness and caution in matters of faith, and by comprehensiveness of belief. Any renewal included all its members or it included none.

Anglican theological method matured during Elizabeth's reign. The distinctive Anglican approach to theology was developed by Richard Hooker (d. 1600) in *The Laws of Ecclesiastical Polity.* In this work, Hooker reflected the characteristic English concern for good institutional governance. According to Hooker, the Anglican method has three elements: Scripture, reason, and tradition. This formulation frequently is labeled "the three-legged stool." The stool needs all three legs to stand. But the legs actually are quite uneven.

Hooker gives utter and complete priority and authority to Scripture. He wrote: "What Scripture doth plainly deliver it is that the first place both of credit and obedience is due; the next whereunto is whatsoever any man can necessarily conclude by force of reason. After these, the voice of the Church succeedeth" (Book V, Chapter 8, Section II). Anglican theology today is guided by this statement.

The Elizabethan Church also set forth the pattern of worship found in many Anglican churches today, the *Book of Common Prayer.* With few changes from the first text in 1549 and the second in 1552, the *Prayer Book* was published in 1559 and restored in 1662 after the Puritan revolt. The *Prayer Book* of Elizabeth's day united the Church of England in a most profound way. The *Book of Common Prayer* in fact means "prayer common to all." After Elizabeth's death, a common Bible was translated for use in the Church, the *Authorized Version* of 1611 (popularly known as the *King James Version*). The authority of Scripture and the use of the *Book of Common Prayer* reveal the Anglican temperament. In no other Church is as much Scripture read or directly incorporated into the form of worship.

For some, the Reformation in England had not gone far enough. The *Book of Common Prayer* and the retention of the ancient threefold order of ministry—bishops, priests, and deacons—were compelling evidence of continuing Roman Catholic influence. Some sought a faith that was a purer reflection of God's will as revealed in Scripture. These people became known as "Puritans." During Elizabeth's stable reign, the Puritan movement increased in size and influence. Puritans followed the teachings of John Calvin and his interpreters. Many Puritan leaders lived and learned in Geneva until it was safe to return to England.

From 1640 to 1658, the Puritans controlled the political and religious life of England. They forced King Charles I from the throne and beheaded him. They purged the Parliament and the Church of any who disagreed with their Calvinist theology and popular politics. Presbyterian polity and belief was instituted for a time. The Westminster Confession, for example, was formulated in 1648. The Revolution, however, began to crumble in the mid to late 1650s and disintegrated completely in 1659. In 1660 the monarchy was reinstated, as were the episcopacy and the *Prayer Book*. The Anglican balance was quickly restored. The Puritan form of Protestantism was a trial for the Anglican soul, which explains the distaste many Episcopalians have for more extreme forms of religion. During the Restoration most Puritans fled to Scotland or to the American colonies, and others recanted and blended in as best they could with the Church of England. Others were imprisoned or put to death when they refused to adhere to the laws of state or Church.

In the eighteenth century, many church leaders and university teachers and scholars were drawn to new scientific developments and to a rational, human-centered understanding of nature. This movement, the Enlightenment, attracted Church leaders from the more traditional Anglican faith to one that more closely approximated deism.[1] This liberal expression of belief made for a spiritually dry period in English church history. The health of souls in the parish churches suffered from profound neglect. Participation in worship, an important indicator of spiritual life, decreased significantly during the period.

In this environment, John and Charles Wesley grew spiritually. By God's grace, they each had profound spiritual experiences which led them to deep personal faith in Christ and a commitment to awaken the Church of England. The official Church hierarchy reacted coldly to these "Methodists" with their emphasis on personal renewal and Christian discipline in prayer, fellowship, and service. There is no question that the Wesleys, both priests of the Church of England, profoundly influenced its course in the latter part of the eighteenth century. At the same time, evangelical renewal was also occurring. No particular circumstance lay behind it. According to Bishop Stephen Neill, writing in his comprehensive work *Anglicanism,* "a surprising number of the early Evangelicals came to their particular tenets through some purely individual experience, related to the Word of God alone, and not to the word of any living man."[2]

Neill also notes differences between the Evangelicals and the Methodists. Evangelicals tended to be Calvinist in orientation, emphasizing the sovereignty of God and the depravity of man, while Methodists were Arminians, emphasizing personal experience of the Holy Spirit, personal holiness, and the perfectibility of man (also called "sanctification"). Evangelicals chose to work in the parish system and through Church hierarchy, whereas Methodists emphasized itinerant preaching and work outside official channels. Evangelicals were Word-centered, while Methodists stressed the importance of the sacrament of Holy Communion.[3]

While some adherents of Methodism broke from the Church of England, the Wesleys did not. Their approach, along with that of the Evangelicals, is part of the scope of renewal in the Anglican tradition. A point on which these movements agreed wholeheartedly was the importance of the fruitfulness of a living faith. Faith had to issue in action. William Wilberforce (d. 1833) embodied this principle of renewal in Anglicanism. He was part of the "Clapham sect," a group of men in politics and government who pressed for evangelical reform. As good Calvinists, they held a theocratic view of the State. The State was an instrument in the hands of God for His will to be accomplished. Therefore, as faithful men, they brought Christian conscience to bear on policies of state. Social evils were not to be tolerated. The abolition of the slave trade, for which Wilberforce worked unstintingly, is but one example of renewal at work in the life of the nation.

Neither Methodists nor Evangelicals expressed much interest in liturgical renewal, most assuredly not of the Roman kind. But there were others of deep faith who sought a recovery of the traditions of the ancient Church (as they understood it), as well as greater ceremony in worship. The Oxford Movement began in 1833, bringing a more Catholic approach to the life of faith and the life of the Church. Among the leaders of the movement was John Henry Newman, a brilliant scholar and a man of deep faith who preached the gospel, yet sought to move behind the Reformation to what he understood as a more authentic and ancient Church. The more he labored for his cause, the more he became convinced that the Roman Church had maintained an unbroken line of apostolic tradition. The Church of England, he believed, had severed itself from this line in Henry VIII's day. So he left the Church of England in 1845 and later became a leading scholar and a cardinal in the Roman Church. But the movement, sometimes called the "Anglo-Catholic movement," remained and exerted a considerable influence in the Church of England. Much of the missionary endeavor in the Episcopal Church can be traced to the priests of the Oxford Movement, who planted many churches in the American wilderness. The Anglo-Catholic principles are still held in many quarters of the denomination. The Anglo-Catholic movement made its chief contribution to renewal in the Episcopal Church in upholding the necessity of sound liturgical worship and a vibrant sacramental life in the Church.

More "mainstream" Anglicans must also be acknowledged for their advocacy of certain theological points. The work of Bishop Charles Gore (d. 1932), contained in a book of essays written by several men entitled *Lux Mundi* (1901), reaffirmed the classic Anglican theological method of Scripture, reason, and tradition, although Gore supported the use of higher criticism in Biblical interpretation. His position is known as "liberal Catholicism." Archbishop William Temple (d. 1918) and, in the United States, William Porcher Dubose (d. 1918) both stressed the centrality of the Incarnation in Anglican theological tradition. Classic Evangelicals focused instead on the Atonement and the doctrine of justification for their principal positions. But Temple and Dubose have deeply influenced the underlying teaching of the Episcopal Church in the twentieth century. Alongside this "liberal Catholicism" has been a "liberal Evangelicalism," centered in the Word but interpreted and guided by human reason and critical exegetical tools.

This quick tour of English church history provides a framework for understanding renewal in the Episcopal Church, and the more particular aspect of evangelical renewal. After all, renewal was not invented by the Episcopal Church in the twentieth century. There is background for it through its Anglican heritage. So often Anglicans are in love with their tradition without knowing its content. That frequently is true for those in the renewal movements in the Episcopal Church.

So we now can summarize that the foundational principles of Anglican theological method are Hooker's triad of Scripture, then reason, then tradition. Reformation principles, particularly the insights of John Calvin, are integrated into the Anglican way. And there is the careful balance of theological position—the Anglican Third Way and the push towards comprehensiveness.

In the eighteenth century, Anglicanism was deeply influenced by Enlightenment principles of science, especially scientific method, rational appreciation of the natural world, and human-centeredness in philosophy and theology. In contrast to this liberal approach, renewal affected the Church of England in three ways: Evangelical/Calvinist, Methodist/Arminian, and Anglo-Catholic. The instrument of renewal of faith in God-in-Christ for each would be, in the above order, the Bible, personal experience, and liturgy.

As we noted, the Oxford Movement profoundly affected the Episcopal Church as it expanded in the American frontier. The Episcopal Church was founded by men of liberal persuasion, given that faith-principles of the Enlightenment shaped the Church of that age. For nearly a century, then, there were two types of Episcopal Churches: the Catholic (or "high church") and the Liberal (or "low church"). While it is true that there were deeply faithful leaders in the Episcopal Church in the mid- to late-nineteenth century, we cannot speak of spiritual renewal in the Episcopal Church until at least the 1920s. There was little motivation, it seemed, for thoroughgoing renewal in the Church. The story of Episcopal renewal is like the story of Episcopal evangelism: the Baptists in this country went out on foot, the Methodists went on horseback, the Presbyterians went by stagecoach, but the Episcopalians waited for the Pullman car.

Historically, evangelicals have exerted minimal impact in the Episcopal Church. During the mid-nineteenth century, some evangelicals left the Church in a dispute with more liberal leaders over liturgical and ceremonial matters, and over the theological interpretation of baptismal regeneration. The *Prayer Book* language suggested to these evangelicals that there was an instantaneous moral change in the one baptized—even when the baptized person was an infant. So they altered the *Prayer Book* language to suit their understanding, omitting all references that could be interpreted to mean complete and instant regeneration. Led by the Rev. Charles E. Cheney of Chicago, and joined by Bishop George D. Cummins of Kentucky, a group numbering about eight thousand five hundred left to form the Reformed Episcopal Church. The Episcopal Church historian James Thayer Addison correctly observed that "they departed not because their own convictions had been declared heretical, but because they thought the Church was not energetic enough in suppressing convictions which they opposed."[4] Evangelical Episcopalians historically have not been at the forefront of renewal in the Church. The formation of the Reformed Episcopal Church is but one example of what some see as the sectarian bent of the evangelicals. It has been rightly said that they are known more for what they have attacked than for what they have affirmed.[5]

The Anglo-Catholic/liberal, high church/low church divisions colored the life of the Episcopal Church through the 1940s. The Church's worship was shaped also by this split, especially in the *Prayer Book* revision of 1928, which sundered the Service of the Word from the Service of the Table. Word and Sacrament have always been balanced in true Anglican tradition, liturgically and theologically. In 1928, the pattern of Morning Prayer for low churchmen and Communion for high churchmen was permitted and set forth in the *Prayer Book*. The evangelicals, small in number, stressed the importance of the Service of the Word because of its focus on Scripture and its exposition in sermons. Unfortunately, evangelicals often were identified with low churchmen in ceremonial battles with the more Catholic-minded, even though the evangelical was defined, not by his point of view of the ceremonial (or lack thereof), but by right preaching of the Word.

Almost as soon as the 1928 *Prayer Book* appeared in the pews, there were calls for further revision. Liturgical revision has had a thorough effect on contemporary forms of renewal in the Episcopal Church. In 1940, the Standing Liturgical Commission of the Episcopal Church was given official authorization to move forward with *Prayer Book* studies and with proposals for a revised liturgy. Beginning in 1918, European Roman Catholic scholars examined the worship of the Church in light of discoveries of ancient Christian liturgical texts. Liturgical theological study simultaneously grew in depth and breadth. Two essential points were set forward from this liturgical study. First, the goal of the Church is to return to the most ancient form and practice of worship, which is regarded as the most authentic expression of apostolic faith. The second point is that liturgy is "the work of the people" rather than the craft of a clerical cadre.

The Episcopal Church, as a liturgical Church, found these insights helpful, and Church leadership embraced this theological approach and liturgical study. The impulse for liturgical renewal and revision led to the founding of Associated Parishes in Washington, D.C., in 1946. Associated Parishes is sometimes identified as a "renewal group," although that is an inaccurate observation. Its work is directed towards revision in worship and revitalization of parish life, rather than to a reformulation of classic Reformation or Patristic theology or practice. Its current project, for example, is inclusive, gender-free language in liturgy and advocacy of an inclusive-language Bible for public reading in parishes.

In any case, liturgical renewal has given form and shape to the prayer life of renewal groups in the Church. A second factor influencing the development of renewal groups in the Church was the Human Potential Movement, which began in Bethel, Maine, in 1947. Grounded in the social psychology of Kurt Lewin, and oriented first to the improvement of organizational life (particularly in business), the Human Potential Movement quickly spread to other fields, including individual psychotherapy and pastoral counseling. The importance of the small group in contemporary parish life can be traced directly to the influence of training models offered by the Human Potential Movement.

The Human Potential Movement first found its way into the seminaries and then into the parishes of the Church through the clergy. An entire generation of Episcopal priests was affected, and continues to be formed, by the Movement's teachings. During the 1950s and 1960s, and even well into the 1970s, for example, the "enabler" model of ministerial leadership dominated clerical life. The role of the priest was to allow the people to become what they were meant to be. The priest was not to direct the "process" of parish life but instead was to "trust the process." Dealing with the feelings that people share with one another was seen to be much more preferable than imparting content. Or, rather, the feelings *are* the content.

Even though the Human Potential Movement is clearly secular in orientation and thoroughly humanistic in its foundations, Episcopal Church leaders uncritically adopted the philosophy and the technique. There is no question that personal relationships were enriched by this movement, but often at the expense of a clear commitment to Christ, consistent theological reflection, and deep and abiding spiritual discipline. Yet there were positive results as well. First, the Church is conceived more and more as "the people of God," each member having gifts for ministry. Secondly, the clerical domination of the Church has been challenged. A healthier view of ordained ministry has given a much more human face to Church leadership and penetrated the mystique of priesthood which so often has blocked renewal in the Church. The conditions were set, then, for the emergence of renewal with a more traditional shape. In its early days, renewal movements defined themselves over against the Human Potential Movement, while using and refining many of the techniques.

During this same period, there were few identifiable renewal figures. One who stands out is the Rev. Samuel Shoemaker (d. 1963), a towering advocate of commitment to Christ and to the evangelistic work of the Church. In his forty-two year ministry, he wrote twenty-eight books, many of them popular best-sellers, assisting people with discovering and deepening their faith. His radio addresses were heard widely and were highly regarded.

While rector of Calvary Church, New York City, Shoemaker began the Faith at Work movement, a lay witnessing fellowship. While rector of Calvary Church, Pittsburgh, he initiated the Pittsburgh Experiment, bringing together labor and management in Christian fellowship and sharing. He was an ardent supporter of the work of Alcoholics Anonymous, especially in its earliest days. He was the guiding force behind the Twelve

Step Program which is the hallmark of A.A.'s approach to recovering from the disease of alcoholism.

Shoemaker would not have labeled himself as an evangelical or a charismatic or a Catholic. He simply preached the gospel, worked intensively in small group leadership training, and worked closely with college students and ordinands in their spiritual formation. Many leaders in contemporary Episcopal renewal owe a deep debt to Shoemaker and his ministry.

Three key contributions of Shoemaker's work shaped future renewal. First, he was convinced of the priority of evangelistic preaching—preaching that leads people to a point of decision about Jesus Christ. In *I Stand by the Door*, his widow, Helen Smith Shoemaker, writes,

> Sam sensed that people are often much more moved than we imagine by preaching and that there should be a strong element of teaching in our modern preaching, for people are spiritually illiterate, and people must have in mind the balance of the Christian message. He believed that all preaching today should be fundamentally evangelistic in intent and that this "Good News" must be presented with conviction, and with clarity, and with passion and compassion.[6]

His preaching drew large crowds both in New York and in Pittsburgh and provoked large numbers of conversions.

Secondly, Shoemaker stressed the fundamental role of the Holy Spirit in Christian faith and life. This was news to the Episcopal Church. In *With the Holy Spirit and with Fire*, he says,

> We who say we believe in the Holy Spirit are capable of far greater achievements than have ever been seen. We know that we cannot command Him, and we know that He alone is capable of creating the world-wide awakening that is needed. But God has always worked through people. It would be difficult to believe that God is not ready to "pour out His Spirit upon all flesh," if only more of us were deeply available to Him. In one sense, awakening is His business alone—in another sense, it is very much up

to us. For while we cannot bring about the awakening in our own strength, we can hold it back by our own refusals.[7]

Shoemaker fervently believed in the power of the Holy Spirit to change cultures, churches (including his own Episcopal Church), as well as individual lives.

Thirdly, he stressed the role of personal witness by the laity. He was among the first to fuse the insights of theological renewal of the Church as the Body of Christ (animated by the Holy Spirit) and the insights of the Human Potential Movement, which emphasized personal sharing and small group experience. Both were the hallmarks of the Faith at Work movement and the Pittsburgh Experiment.

Faith at Work was incorporated in 1953 and grew out of Shoemaker's ministry at Calvary Church in New York City. It was meant to be an ecumenical group sharing how Christ was changing the whole lives of the members. Participants shared the difficult business and personal decisions they had to make, and other participants supported them and prayed for and with them. Real Christian discipleship and community thereby were experienced. The Pittsburgh Experiment developed into an ecumenical prayer group and Bible study with business people and labor officials meeting at various offices in downtown Pittsburgh.

Faith at Work ceased as an organization in 1977. The Pittsburgh Experiment continues today to be a viable organization meeting for prayer, Christian discipleship, and mutual understanding. One other little-known fact about Shoemaker should be added here regarding his ministry with college students. He was one of the founders of Campus Crusade for Christ. His vision of renewal was indeed broad in reach and deep in influence.

Shoemaker's story shows how God can work through one person to affect profoundly the awakening of the wider Episcopal Church. His attention to the work of the Holy Spirit paralleled the emergence of the charismatic movement in the Episcopal Church. While Pentecostalism has been around for some time, the charismatic movement in the Episcopal Church can be traced only to the late 1950s. In 1957 at Trinity Church in

Wheaton, Illinois, then-rector Richard Winkler and several members of the congregation manifested the Holy Spirit through extraordinary healings and glossolalia (speaking in tongues). The event caused such a stir that it was featured in *Time* magazine. Another outpouring of the Holy Spirit occurred through the healing ministry of the Rev. Dennis Bennett at St. Mark's, Van Nuys, California. And at about the same time the Rev. Graham Pulkingham at Church of the Redeemer in Houston also experienced this outpouring of the Spirit which, in that parish's case, resulted in strong community building within and significant community ministry beyond the parish.

Since the 1960s, the charismatic movement has gained greater acceptance in the Episcopal Church. Perhaps 15 to 20 percent of the clergy are identified with the charismatic movement, and 10 to 15 percent of the parishes. The strong emphasis on healing has made the movement more acceptable to mainstream Episcopalians.[8] A principal weakness of the movement has been its strong emphasis on personal experience to the exclusion of those who have not had "the baptism of the Holy Spirit." Those who have not had some kind of Pentecostal experience are viewed as spiritually incomplete. Such attitudes can be divisive in parish life, rather than renewing. In addition, far more attention has been given to personal piety than to social concern. Finally, the charismatic movement is an experience looking for a theology. It has not been grounded carefully and deeply in Biblically-based doctrine and authority. As the movement matures, this last problem will no doubt be addressed.

So it is by now evident that there are three "streams" of renewal in the contemporary Episcopal Church: the Anglo-Catholic, the evangelical, and the charismatic. Each has a distinct history and slant in the Church. The difference can be outlined this way. If one were to ask, "How does a person come to know Jesus Christ as Lord and Savior?" the Anglo-Catholic would answer, "Through liturgy and sacrament." The evangelical would answer, "Through reading and hearing God's Word." The charismatic would respond, "Through a recognizable experience of the Holy Spirit."

The first time that the leaders of these three streams of renewal were brought together in any organized way was at

"The 3Rs Conference" held in January 1986 in Winter Park, Florida. In that conference, participants addressed the fundamentals of faith for Episcopalians. The "3Rs" stand for "The Revelation of God, the Renewal of the Church, and the Reformation of Society." These are the three components of authentic renewal in the Church as Episcopalians understand them. We discovered that we could affirm a significant body of doctrine in common, beginning with the assertion that Christ is the Head of the Church. It was, in the words of Dr. J. I. Packer, the prominent Anglican theologian, "the convergence of the saints."

The renewal of the Church, as we learned together in the Conference, is not novelty, nor institutional program, nor revival. The renewal of the Church is dependent upon Jesus Christ, the Risen Lord. As Dr. Packer and Bishop Michael Marshall, the Anglican evangelist, have stated:

> As for renewal, the Spirit has shown us that where, in accordance with the Scriptures, Jesus Christ is known, trusted, loved, and adored as Savior, Master, and Friend; where all forms of sin are hated and renounced; where Christ's living presence is sought and found in the fellowship of his people; and where action is ruled by the passion to do righteousness, to make others great before God, and thus to glorify our glorious Lord; there the church is in renewal, in whatever variety of liturgical and devotional forms the new life finds expression. It is obedience to the Lordship of Christ that gives authority to the preaching of the gospel and the witness of the church. Renewal begins as obedience is recovered.[9]

The entire statement "Our Testimony Today" (from which this portion is drawn) was adopted with unanimous acclaim by the one hundred participants. We agreed that "our experience of the presence and power of the Lord in this conference, showing us his truth and pouring out upon us his Spirit within our converging flames of renewal, has led us to resolve that for the future, we will pursue renewal in the Episcopal Church, not separately, but together."[10] No one group "owns" renewal, but all contribute to a full understanding of it in personal lives and in the Church at large. When renewal is consistent with the

Anglican tradition, it does contain three elements: catholic worship (Word *and* sacrament), evangelical witness, and charismatic power. Renewal is explicitly grounded in worship of a holy and sovereign God and in the fruit of repentance before Him.

Our unity in renewal does not mean that we do away with distinctives. We each have a different approach to the same truth and realize that we need the contributions of the others for a holistic approach to renewal. Of course, there are those in each stream of renewal who believe that their approach is the only way for renewal to take place, while attacking other approaches and ridiculing them. Sectarian strife, as we have noted, is one result of renewal in the experience of Anglicans. But when we are authentic instruments of the Spirit's renewing work, we cannot have a party spirit about us. We learn from and celebrate one another's distinctiveness and strengths.

What, then, are the distinctives today of the evangelical approach to renewal in the Anglican tradition? A study of the evangelical movement in the Episcopal Church has yet to be written, in part because the evangelical impulse, as we have noted, is not much in evidence before 1960. But we can note the following traits.

First, the evangelical in the Anglican tradition upholds the primacy and unremitting authority of Scripture for the Christian. The evangelical is squarely within Anglican tradition, as we have seen. The evangelical also concurs with Article VI of the Thirty-Nine Articles (guidelines for Anglican faith agreed upon in 1571): "Holy Scripture containeth all things necessary to salvation; so that whatsoever is not read therein, nor may be proved thereby, is not to be required of any man, that it should be believed as an article of the Faith, or be thought requisite or necessary to salvation." The evangelical would add that Scripture is to be regarded as *infallible* with regard to faith and morals. God's Word stands firm in all ages and for all people. The Anglican evangelical looks critically at "higher criticism" and uses those tools simply to get a clearer grasp of what Scripture may be teaching at a certain point.

The 3Rs Conference on the Priority of Preaching restated a classic evangelical conviction. The exposition, study, and preaching of God's Word are essential to the presence of Christ in the Church and in human lives. Evangelicals are people who believe passionately in the gospel and who are committed to share the Good News of salvation in Jesus Christ. The Spirit works through the Scriptures to affect the lives of those who hear. The Conference Committee wrote:

> Preaching has authority when it takes us to the God of the Bible. It has the power to convey salvation by establishing a connection between God's love, judgment, and mercy and the minds and hearts of a congregation. The preacher must have experienced this life-changing power, must be a biblical person submitted to Jesus Christ as he is revealed in the Scriptures, and must be convinced of the urgency and authority of this task.[11]

Personal conversion and holiness of life are key elements in effective communication of God's Word. The ordained ministers need the life-changing power that God alone can give, something John Wesley had been saying nearly two hundred years before.

The Anglican evangelical is convinced that all humans need salvation by faith alone through the unmerited grace of God. There is no way a person can be saved outside of acknowledging his or her sinfulness and coming before God trusting in His abundant mercy. Salvation is received, not achieved. That principle has not always been well understood in Anglicanism. Something of the Pelagian heresy remains.[12] Some Anglican evangelicals would agree with Calvin that human beings are totally and utterly depraved. Others would affirm that there is some residue of goodness in human beings which can never be rightly expressed outside a saving relationship with Christ. In this view, human beings are deeply and profoundly warped and marred from God's original intent and design.

The Church, in the evangelical view, is the Body of Christ, and it is the community and the fellowship of the saved. The Church witnesses to the saving relationship that all people can have with God in Jesus Christ. The Church's primary tasks are to witness and to convert, to bear the gospel wherever and whenever possible. It is first a herald to the world and then a fellowship of Christians gathered together for sacramental worship and faithful service.

The evangelical Anglican stresses that God's work with His

creation is not yet finished. The Lord Jesus Christ will come again, just as He left. In contrast to the liberal view, the evangelical believes in the personal return of Jesus Christ to complete the work of salvation. Liberals say instead that this eschatological hope has already been realized and accomplished in the resurrection. The Anglican evangelical would respond that the entire New Testament points to a firm hope in the conclusion of all history under the Lordship of Christ. Jesus must return to finish the work He has already begun. This anticipation fuels the evangelical's desire to share the Good News.[13]

Episcopal evangelicals are deeply indebted to Anglican evangelicals who came to theological maturity in the years immediately following World War II. As we have noted, the evangelical movement has a long history in the Church of England. With the rise of the Student Christian Movement (later to become InterVarsity Christian Fellowship), these Anglican evangelicals developed two contemporary characteristics out of their long history: a focus on the authority of the Bible and a vision for world mission. Five names stand out clearly: John R. W. Stott, J. I. Packer, Bishop Stephen Neill, Bryan Green, and Michael Green (no relation). Each of these men has left his mark on countless American students, many of them Episcopal, who have visited or studied overseas or, in Stott's and Packer's case, heard them in America.

The Rev. Peter Moore, now rector of Little Trinity Church in Toronto, Ontario, was one of the early indigenous evangelicals in the Episcopal Church. Another was the Rev. Fitzsimmons Allison, for many years professor of church history at the seminary of the University of the South in Sewanee, Tennessee, and then at Virginia Theological Seminary. Allison currently is bishop of South Carolina. A third early evangelical was the Rev. John H. Rodgers, Jr., for many years professor of systematic theology at Virginia Theological Seminary and now dean of Trinity Episcopal School for Ministry in Ambridge, Pennsylvania.

Moore believes that the key to the development of a viable evangelical movement in this country was the arrival in 1963 of the Rev. Philip Edgecombe Hughes, the New Testament scholar.[14] He, along with the Very Rev. Stuart Barton Babbage, formerly dean of Melbourne Cathedral, Australia, and a colleague at Columbia Seminary, brought an evangelical witness to bear wherever they spoke in the Episcopal Church. They helped Moore to identify the isolated Episcopal evangelicals. They also encouraged the Episcopal evangelicals' association with the Evangelical Fellowship in the Anglican Communion (EFAC), the international body of Anglican evangelicals. Through this association, many Anglican evangelicals were brought to this country. Beginning in the mid-1960s in Pawling, New York, a series of conferences began which strengthened the contacts between Episcopal evangelicals and their English and Australian counterparts. Then, in 1966, the first official evangelical gathering in this country took place at St. James' Church in Leesburg, Virginia, under the direction of its evangelical rector, Peter Doyle. Stott, Hughes, Rodgers, and Allison all played a role in the conference. Out of it began the evangelical voice in the Episcopal Church, the Fellowship of Witness.

The Fellowship of Witness took on new vitality and stronger organization under the direction of the Rev. John Guest, rector of St. Stephen's Church, Sewickley, Pennsylvania. Guest, an Englishman, arrived in the United States as youth missioner of Scripture Union in Philadelphia in 1966. He then became the college coordinator for the Pittsburgh Experiment in 1968, and in 1969 he became youth minister at St. Stephen's. In 1970, he was called to become the rector. With evangelical fervor and evangelistic dynamism, the parish grew rapidly under his leadership and became a center for evangelical development in the United States.

In 1970, a meeting of evangelical clergy took place at St. Stephen's to chart the course of evangelical renewal. At this meeting, the Fellowship of Witness grew stronger. The magazine *Kerygma* grew out of this meeting. A strategy was developed for the furtherance of the evangelical movement, including one key vision: the development of an evangelical, renewal-oriented seminary to train not only ordained clergy, but also lay leaders. Thus, Trinity Episcopal School for Ministry was born, and its doors opened under the administration of Bishop Alfred Stanway, an Australian, in 1976. The seminary has prospered against great odds and has grown into a respected institution for the training of men and women for many forms of ministry. It has helped to insure the long-term viability of the evangelical movement in the Episcopal Church.

The Church's other eleven seminaries have been admitting

increasing numbers of Episcopal evangelicals, or those influenced by the movement. The coming generation of clergy in the Episcopal Church promises to be far more enthusiastic about personal and parish renewal than many of their liberal forebearers. As is so often the case, the laity have been in the forefront, touched by the ministry of Billy Graham, Robert Schuller, and other Protestant evangelists. Still others have been moved by the testimony of bishops, clergy, and laity from East Africa, where evangelical renewal has been occurring for some time, particularly under the leadership of Bishop Festo Kivengere in Uganda. It may well be the African Anglicans who will ultimately evangelize jaded Episcopalians in the United States.

Evangelical and other major renewal movements have yet to make any major impact upon the institutional Episcopal Church. But the time is coming. If those motivated by renewal press for leadership in the Episcopal Church, a major hurdle will be passed. There will be a much stronger hope for the future of the Episcopal Church. During the last twenty years, denominational membership has declined precipitously. By some estimates, membership has shrunk by 20 percent. Much of this membership loss can be laid squarely upon the reckless social theology and advocacy embedded in secular humanistic philosophy which affected the Episcopal Church in the 1950s and 1960s. Now this membership decline seems to have halted, and the Church appears numerically stable. Where parishes are growing, there is renewal, be it Anglo-Catholic, evangelical, or charismatic renewal. Where Christ is head, the faithful will multiply. Bishop Alden Hathaway of Pittsburgh, a leading evangelical in the church, has asserted, "We must claim for renewal the recent turnaround in membership and stewardship in the Episcopal Church, reversing the downward slide of the last twenty-five years." That is not triumphalistic boasting. That is the reality of the Episcopal Church today.

Evangelical renewal is but one element in the overall pattern of renewal in the Episcopal Church. While it has its distinctive theological approach, it is open to others who claim Jesus as Lord and Head of the Church. Evangelical renewal is true to the Anglican tradition. It holds to doctrine as received by the Church and based in the authority of Scripture; to discipline, as faithfully practiced and evangelistically pursued; and to worship, as found in the *Book of Common Prayer* in its contemporary expression in the Episcopal Church. Evangelical renewal is faithful to its Reformation heritage, but with the particular Anglican flavor of comprehensiveness, clarity of thought, and pure devotion to Jesus Christ.

A DIRECTORY OF RENEWAL GROUPS AND PUBLICATIONS IN THE EPISCOPAL CHURCH

Fellowship of Witness is an evangelical organization dedicated to education and fellowship. It holds yearly preaching conferences. More information is available from its secretary, The Rev. James Basinger, Rector, St. Francis Episcopal Church, 432 Forest Hill Road, Macon, Georgia 30210.

Trinity Episcopal School for Ministry is a seminary for laity who may or may not be seeking ordination. It is evangelically-oriented. More information is available from the Very Rev. John H. Rodgers, Jr., Dean/President, TESM, 311 Eleventh Street, Ambridge, Pennsylvania 15003. It also publishes a journal entitled *Mission and Ministry.* Direct inquiries to the Editor, the Rev. Samuel Abbott, Rector, St. James Episcopal Church, 1991 Massachusetts Avenue, Cambridge, Massachusetts 02140.

Brotherhood of St. Andrew is a ministry for men and young people which has, as its purpose, "to spread Christ and his Kingdom." For information, write the executive director at 109 Merchant Street, P.O. Box 532, Ambridge, Pennsylvania 15003.

The Church Army is an organization dedicated to evangelism and mission. Write for more information c/o The Episcopal Church Center, 815 Second Avenue, New York, New York 10017.

Episcopal Center for Evangelism is organized to promote renewal and evangelism in the Episcopal Church and to produce a wide range of material for the same. Write c/o The Very Rev. Robert B. Hall, Executive Director, Box 920, Live Oak, Florida 32060.

Pewsaction is an umbrella organization dedicated to Episcopal renewal. They run the biennial Ridgecrest Conference. For more information, contact Mrs. Ivan Merrick, Chairman, 1000 8th Avenue, A-1001, Seattle, Washington, 98104.

Episcopal Renewal Ministries is the umbrella for charismatic renewal in the Episcopal Church. For more information, contact The Rev. Charles M. Irish, Executive Director, 10520 Main Street, Fairfax, Virginia 22030.

The following are identified world mission organizations which promote evangelical renewal and provide opportunities for ministry and service:

CMJ/USA, the Church Mission to the Jews, the American branch of this English ministry to Jewish people. Contact The Rev. Philip Bottomley, Executive Director, Suite 201, 1402 Shepard Drive, Sterling, Virginia 22170.

Episcopal Church Missionary Community trains for the mission field and does mission awareness workshops in parishes. Contact The Rev. Walter Hannum, Executive Director, 1567 Elizabeth Street, Pasadena, California 91104.

Episcopal World Mission, training for global missions. The executive director also conducts preaching missions. Contact Mr. Paul Walter, Executive Director, Box 490, Forest City, North Carolina 28043.

SAMS/USA, the American branch of South American Missionary Society, training for South and Central America. Contact the Rev. Canon Derek Hawksbee, Executive Director, Box 276, Union Mills, North Carolina 28167.

SPCK/USA is the American branch of the English publishing and evangelistic society. The Rev. Richard Kew is the American director. Write c/o SPO Box 1103, Sewanee, Tennessee 37375.

SOMA, Sharing of Ministries Abroad, provides short-term overseas missions experiences and brings Third World church leaders to the United States. Write c/o The Rev. F. Brian Cox, IV, Church of the Apostles, Box 2306, Fairfax, Virginia 22031.

The following are evangelistic organizations or individuals engaged in evangelistic ministry.

Adventures in Faith is the renewal ministry of Edwin and Joyce Neville, who conduct parish renewal weekends. Write c/o 175 Bryant Street, Buffalo, New York 14222.

Faith Alive is an organization which conducts parish renewal weekends which especially emphasize lay witness in the parish. Write c/o Mr. Fred C. Gore, President, P.O. Box 1987, York, Pennsylvania 17405.

New Life Ministries is the evangelistic crusade ministry of the Rev. John Guest. Write c/o St. Stephen's Episcopal Church, Frederick Avenue, Sewickley, Pennsylvania 15143.

The Rev. Charles Murphy and his wife, Anne, conduct evangelistic missions and retreat weekends. Write c/o 1015 Danville Road, S.W., Decatur, Alabama 35601.

The Rev. John R. Throop coordinated The 3Rs Conference in Winter Park, Florida, and will coordinate the Conference on Conversion in the Anglican Tradition in Sewanee, Tennessee, in 1987. He is available for evangelism events and retreats. Write c/o Christ Episcopal Church, 3445 Warrensville Center Road, Shaker Heights, Ohio 44122.

DR. WALDO J. WERNING

is an adjunct professor and seminary relations officer at Concordia Theological Seminary, Fort Wayne, Indiana. Over a period of twenty-five years, he was stewardship executive for the Lutheran Church—Missouri Synod in several states as well as in the St. Louis headquarters of the denomination. He has held various positions with denominational agencies. He is the author of several works, including *The Radical Nature of Christianity* and *Vision and Strategy for Church Growth*.

THREE

The Lutheran Churches

Waldo J. Werning

T he Lutheran churches in America experienced a dramatic increase in numbers as a result of the large influx of immigrants in the late nineteenth and early twentieth centuries. Large numbers of those immigrants came from heavily Lutheran countries such as Germany and the Scandanavian nations. A number of factors kept those early Lutherans divided. For one thing, even though they were Lutherans, they had different national roots, languages, and customs. They also settled in widely separated parts of America.

As many as one hundred and fifty different Lutheran bodies once existed in the United States. By the mid-1980s—because of numerous mergers—95 percent of American Lutherans were members of one of three groups: the American Lutheran Church, the Lutheran Church in America, or the Lutheran Church—Missouri Synod. The American Lutheran Church came into being in 1960 as a merger of the American Lutheran Church (primarily Lutherans of German descent), the Evangelical Lutheran Church (Norwegian), and the United Evangelical Lutheran Church (Danish). The Lutheran Church in America resulted from a 1962 merger of the United Lutheran Church in America, the American Evangelical Lutheran Church, the Finnish Evangelical Lutheran Church, and the Augustana Evangelical Lutheran Church. The Lutheran Church—Missouri Synod dates back to 1847. These three Lutheran bodies were relatively similar in size. The Lutheran Church in America, with 2.9 million members, was the largest, while the American Lutheran Church (2.3 million) was the smallest. The Lutheran Church—Missouri Synod (2.6 million) was second in size. The next largest Lutheran body is the Wisconsin Evangelical Lutheran Synod with four hundred thousand members.

No knowledgeable person would deny that of the three largest Lutheran groups, the most theologically liberal was the Lutheran Church in America. Nor would such a person reject the claim that the Lutheran Church—Missouri Synod was the most conservative. Theological orthodoxy was a special concern of Missouri Synod Lutherans from the very start. Most of the people who began what became the Missouri Synod were Germans who had fought theological liberalism in the homeland. Many came to America to seek religious freedom and organize a synod that would recognize the sovereignty of the local congregation.

On January 1, 1988, the Lutheran Church in America, the American Lutheran Church, and a much smaller body, the Association of Evangelical Lutheran Churches, expect to complete a merger that will unite them in the Evangelical Lutheran Church in America. The 5.3 million members of the new Lutheran body will then compose approximately 60 percent of all Lutherans in America. The new large denomination's openness to liberal theological views will remain unacceptable to most Missouri Synod Lutherans. The new denomination will also be open to ecumenical cooperation that too often appears to ignore essential doctrinal considerations that Missouri Synod Lutherans are unwilling to surrender. Obviously, any claim like this is a generalization. There are many theological conservatives in the new denomination, and the Missouri Synod has more than its share of theological liberals. But the theological differences between the two Lutheran bodies is an important factor in understanding the nature of evangelical renewal in American Lutheranism.

As other chapters in this book explain, evangelical renewal is an attempt to deal with three separate problems in a denomination. The first of these is doctrinal renewal. When a denomination turns its back on the purity of the New Testament gospel, it offers what is, in effect, a substitute for New Testament Christianity. Lutherans have long been champions of orthodoxy, as anyone can quickly see by examining the importance they have attached to church confessions. When leaders of a Church deny that Jesus Christ is the eternal Son of God whose death was an atonement for the sins of a fallen race, when they deny the resurrection of Christ, when they repudiate the inspiration and infallibility of the Holy Scriptures, then it is time for Biblically-informed Lutherans to become involved in doctrinal renewal.

But evangelical renewal involves more than a concern with doctrine; it is also concerned with bringing men and women to recognize and acknowledge that their only hope for heaven is the finished work of the Lord Jesus Christ. American Lutheranism is no different from other mainline denominations with regard to the fact that many who need evangelizing today are nominal members of their own churches.

Finally, evangelical renewal means challenging spiritually lethargic or dead Christians to become revived and renewed in their commitment to Bible study, Christian living, evangelism, and discipling. American Lutheranism is fertile territory for this last work of renewal.

THE NEED FOR RENEWAL

In 1972 the Augsburg Publishing Company issued a book titled *A Study of Generations* that provided an interesting and informative look at Lutheran values, beliefs, and practices.[1] While polling techniques are always subject to minor variations and while the book was produced in an earlier decade, its picture of American Lutheranism is still accurate enough to allow certain conclusions to be drawn. If nothing else, the statistical information in the book points to the need for evangelical renewal in American Lutheranism.

Take the matter of doctrine, for example. The book presents statistics showing that 30 percent of Lutherans have doubts about the deity of Jesus Christ. About 40 percent have doubts about the existence of God.[2] Twenty-five percent of the Lutherans who were polled rejected the Trinity; 33 percent doubted that Jesus was perfect in every way; and 31 percent doubted that Jesus was even alive today.[3] The survey indicates that large pockets of Lutherans have doubts about the virgin birth and bodily resurrection of Jesus. Thirty-six percent hold neoorthodox or liberal attitudes towards the Bible.[4]

More than doctrine is at stake in these widely held doubts. When anyone denies that Jesus is the eternal Son of God, that Jesus rose from the dead, and that Jesus Christ lives today, it is difficult to see how such a person can properly be regarded as a Christian in the New Testament sense of the word (1 Corinthians 15:1-4; Romans 10:9, 10).

Each person polled was asked to respond to the following sentences: "Jesus Christ died for sinners. As a substitute, he suffered the just penalty due us for our sins in order to satisfy the wrath of God and to save guilty men from hell." Only about 50 percent of the polled Lutherans agreed with this Biblical ground for human salvation.[5] Seventy-two percent believed that most world religions lead to the same God, while 44 percent believed that salvation depends on simply being sincere in whatever you believe. Fifty-nine percent thought that the main emphasis of the gospel is on God's rules for right living.[6]

It would be difficult to imagine a set of claims more in conflict with historic Lutheran principles. I refer to the central Lutheran conviction that justification comes by faith alone and thus that human good works cannot save. I refer as well to the Lutheran belief that salvation is to be found in Jesus Christ alone; Christ and Christ alone is the Way, the Truth, and the Life! Even the editors of the volume concluded that perhaps 40 percent of all Lutherans have no clear understanding of the gospel and are prone to the heresy of Pelagianism.[7]

Only 46 percent of the polled Lutherans were certain of being saved in Christ.[8] Seventy-nine percent said that doing good for others is either absolutely necessary for salvation or would help towards one's salvation.[9] The survey also made it clear that relatively few Lutherans do much in the way of personal evangelism.[10] What the book made clear is that anyone genuinely interested in the cause of evangelical renewal in America's mainline Churches would be justified in regarding American Lutheranism as a mission field.

What the aforementioned statistics fail to reveal is the much greater concentration of doctrinal deviance among many leaders of the Lutheran bodies, including their theologians and Bible professors, to say nothing of many of their pastors. Many Lutheran seminary professors have capitulated to the views of such German Lutherans as Rudolf Bultmann. They reject the inspiration, infallibility, and authority of the Scriptures; they deny the historical accuracy of the Biblical picture of Jesus; and they ridicule such essential tenets of historic Christianity as the Trinity, the deity of Christ, the Incarnation, and the resurrection of Christ. For many Lutheran leaders today, the proclamation of the gospel is replaced by a liberal social agenda that includes the defense of abortion-on-demand and homosexuality. A growing number of Lutheran leaders accept the universalist belief that all human beings will eventually be saved.

Several years ago the leadership of the American Lutheran Church presented *The Evangelical Catechism* as a model in communicating the Christian faith. The *Catechism* fails to take a confessional stance regarding the virgin birth of Jesus, the resurrection, the miracles which Jesus performed, the Trinity, and the deity of the Holy Spirit, whom the *Catechism* refers to only as a "power." The *Catechism's* teaching about a personal devil, real angels, original sin, and the authority of Scripture is out of step with what the Scriptures and the Lutheran Confessions clearly teach and confess. Rather than oppose the spirit of our day, the *Catechism* capitulates to it.

But I offer the ALC *Catechism* as only one of many examples that could be given. Serious theological problems afflict all the major branches of American Lutheranism. American Lutheranism has more serious difficulties than its members realize or its leaders care to admit. It is time that Lutherans take more seriously their rich doctrinal heritage.

But as the statistics cited earlier indicate, Lutheran congregations also need to acknowledge the deep spiritual problems that exist in many local churches. Many Lutherans know little about the Bible. Sixty to 70 percent of American Lutherans do not worship during any given week. Many Lutherans think of their church only as an institution to be maintained and protected; they fail to see it as an important instrument through which God's work can be done. Many Lutherans sense that things are wrong but do not know the combination to the lock that can open the door to renewal.

A LUTHERAN MODEL OF RENEWAL

What is an authentic model of renewal from a Lutheran perspective? With what should Lutherans concern themselves as they commit themselves to evangelical renewal?

Since renewal is a work of God, it must always be dependent on Him. God renews His people through the Word and sacraments by the Holy Spirit; renewal must always be centered on Jesus Christ as Savior and Lord. Renewal should be a normal part of the Christian life. To be renewed is to be kept strong or to be brought back to full commitment to the Triune God.

Biblical history shows that renewal rests on a clear and powerful proclamation of the prophetic Word of God that brings people to an awareness of their spiritual decline, along with their need for a closer walk with God. Renewal in the Bible was marked by genuine worship of God and the destruction of idols that kept people from acknowledging Him as the true and living Lord. Repentance of sin and separation from its control were followed by forgiveness which in turn led to unbounded gladness and the joy of great service to God.

The basic conditions for renewal include an awareness of the existence of God as Creator along with an understanding of God's holiness, justice, and love; an understanding of who Jesus Christ is and why He became incarnate, died, and rose again; a personal faith in the Lord Jesus Christ whose death and resurrection is the only ground of human salvation accompanied by repentance of sin; and the full and free forgiveness in Christ that accompanies an acceptance of the gospel. This justification of the believer must then be followed by sanctification, the process by which the Holy Spirit helps us to grow in personal holiness.

Biblical renewal means that Lutherans will not settle for merely being Christians "in theory" but will become aware of God's involvement in every area of their lives. Biblical renewal results in Christian's being able to speak freely to others about the crucified and resurrected Christ, express love for each other, and speak naturally and freely to God in prayer.

THE ELEMENTS OF RENEWAL

It is possible to explain evangelical renewal more fully in terms of a number of basic steps that must be taken before individual Christians, their local congregations, and their denomination can be all that God expects them to be.

1) Lutherans must work to recover a high view of Scripture. Pastors who hold a high view of Scripture should find ways of acquainting their parishioners with the various ways in

which the authority and infallibility of the Bible are being attacked in the denomination. Members of the Church should be provided with literature that will help them understand the issues. In many Lutheran churches these days, the laypeople hold a higher view of Scripture than the pastor. Laypeople should become acquainted with the issues on their own in such cases. Such laypeople may find it helpful to visit Christian bookstores and become acquainted with literature that may help them become more informed.[11] They should not hesitate to inquire into their pastor's views about the Bible.

Where pastor and church are united in their commitment to a high view of Scripture, they should seek ways of influencing other churches; they should be vocal in expressing their concerns at the denominational level.

2) Lutherans should become informed about the rejection of essential Christian doctrines in their denomination and work to bring about a return to sound doctrine. When Lutherans discover that their denominational leaders are more concerned about defending the practices of homosexuals and killing the unborn than they are about proclaiming the New Testament gospel, they should stop being silent. Evangelical Lutheran laypeople and pastors are helping to support financially many seminaries, colleges, and agencies that undercut the doctrinal integrity of contemporary Lutheranism. Some may wish to consider whether such use of their money expresses faithfulness to the God whose gospel is being denied.

3) Evangelical renewal also has an essential experiential side. Lutherans need to repent and experience forgiveness in Christ, sustained by the means of grace and aided by intense prayer.

4) Lutherans must recognize Jesus Christ as the Head of the Church, which is His Body; they must acknowledge God as Father and Creator, the One to whom we are responsible for all we do; and they must recover a Biblical view of the Holy Spirit whose spiritual gifts equip Christians for the building up of the Body of Christ (Ephesians 4:12, 16).

5) Lutherans must realize that parish renewal begins with personal renewal; only strong Christians can be God's effective tools for renewal in the Church.

6) Lutherans need to remember that renewal involves a

struggle, as Christians are aided by Christ to experience the victory of the new man over the old man (Galatians 5:16-25; 2:20).

7) Lutherans should give more attention to Paul's words in 2 Timothy 2:2—"And the things you have heard me say in the presence of many witnesses entrust to reliable men who will also be qualified to teach others." Renewal spreads as pastors disciple leaders who then disciple others. Each congregation should be a school to make disciples, teaching them to observe the things Christ has commanded. Lutherans should become involved in the process of building each other up in the faith by speaking the Word of Law and Gospel to each other. Each church should lead its members into planned Bible study.

8) The family has an important role to play in renewal. Lutherans should work at the renewal of the Christian family through family Bible study and worship.

9) Lutherans need to give renewed emphasis to the priesthood of all believers (1 Peter 2:9) and the ministry of every member (Ephesians 4:12). As the shepherd of the flock, pastors should be concerned to equip the members of their congregations to minister to others. More attention should be given to serving others inside and outside of the Church; Lutherans should be taught that it is more important to serve than to be served.

10) Inner renewal will manifest itself in evangelism and missions as Lutherans share Jesus Christ through witness and planned evangelism with those who do not know Him. This includes reaching delinquent and inactive members of Lutheran churches. As increasing numbers of Lutherans discover their gifts and as congregations discover new ways of aiding people (both inside and outside the Church) spiritually and materially, new ministries may well develop.

THE GOD OF JUSTICE AND LOVE

Lutherans need to recover an understanding of God's holiness, justice, and love. When Lutherans truly understand the doctrine of the God of justice and love, they will gain a fuller picture of the law and gospel, the old man and the new man, repentance and forgiveness. All of these are important emphases of Scripture and focal points of Lutheran theology. Yet studies indicate that over half of all contemporary Lutherans lack a clear understanding or working knowledge of the God of justice and love, law and gospel, the old man and the new man. Repentance and forgiveness are far too shallow at the moment to ground any hope for real renewal. In fact, less than half of all Lutherans today are entirely certain of their salvation. Believers need to know that God's justice has been fulfilled by His love which made the salvation of all humankind possible through the sacrifice of Jesus Christ on the Cross.

Lutheran theology emphasizes the need to understand life under grace in which believers face both law and gospel. The law is an X-ray or mirror as it judges, condemns, and exposes idolatry; it curbs sinful acts and reveals our efforts to hide our sin; it is also a guide to the will of God; it prepares the heart for the gospel. The gospel declares forgiveness and provides assurance that our guilt has been removed; this in turn provides inner healing. The power of forgiveness leads to good works, warms the heart, lights the path, and gives joy. The distinction between law and gospel is an important precondition for understanding the Bible and living the Christian life. No one was ever saved by law but only by grace. Works are not the means of salvation but the result of it.

The believer needs to know who he or she is—both old man (sinner) and new man (saint). The old nature or old self is ignorant, arrogant, undisciplined, haughty, shameless, disobedient; it doubts God's Word, lives for self, and craves worldly benefits; it is a willing slave of the Devil and has the mind of sin. The new nature or new self is Christ-centered, aware of the truth, renewed in the mind, alive to Christ, dead to the world, obedient, humble, pious, and disciplined. Such texts as Galatians 5:19-22 and Ephesians 4:22-24 tell us to put off the works of the flesh and to put on the fruit of the Spirit. There is a civil war going on in the heart and mind of every believer, but victory is assured by the Holy Spirit who helps the new man triumph over the old man. The precondition for such victory, however, is the believer's surrender to Christ (Galatians 2:20).

Repentance and forgiveness are central to the life of the Christian as well as to the congregation. This truth is especially important at a time when church members are too often influenced by a tolerant culture that refuses to acknowledge sin as sin. A lack of repentance among members has made many congregations impotent in the face of a materialistic and self-indulgent world.

SACRAMENTAL INTEGRITY

Lutherans historically have differed from many evangelicals in their view of the sacraments. Therefore, whatever evangelical renewal will mean in a Lutheran context, it will have to be faithful to the Lutheran understanding of the sacraments.

Lutherans believe there are three means of grace "by which Jesus comes to minister to us."[12] They are the Word and the two sacraments: baptism and the Lord's Supper. As two Lutheran authors explain, "The Holy Spirit, who was poured out on Pentecost works through these means, so that Christ comes to us now—not immediately (or directly) as in the days of His flesh, but mediately (or indirectly) in these times of the Spirit. It is the Spirit who unites women and men to Christ through Word and sacrament."[13]

True Lutherans will never denigrate the Holy Scriptures as a means through which Christ comes to us. But, as our authors explain, "Events also communicate His presence, pardon, and power. Lutherans believe there are two such repeatable actions that manifest Christ to us—baptism and the Lord's Supper."[14] While some of our evangelical friends have made the sacraments seem to be a response to the Lord (law), Lutherans have correctly viewed them as God's action toward man (gospel, grace). These sacred acts are instruments through which God does His work in the hearts of believers. Baptism and the Lord's Supper are involved with the mystery of the gospel. Of course, many Lutherans need to be reminded that the sacraments are not rites that work in some automatic mechanical way; they receive their efficacy through the Word of God as the Holy Spirit brings us to faith.

CONFESSIONAL PURITY

Like any confessional Church, the Lutheran Church sometimes falls into the habit of merely reciting the faith it has inherited. A renewed Lutheranism will be a confessing Church that boldly witnesses to its faith and, in the process, purifies both its faith and its practices. Without confessional purity, it is difficult to see how any Church can witness against the idolatry and false ideologies of the day or contrast the true faith with heresy and paganism. Many Lutherans need to recover the fullness of their Lutheran tradition. Given the inroads of unbelief and doctrinal deviance, what Lutheranism needs today is a new Reformation that will break with the errors of our day as the Reformers of the sixteenth century did with theirs.

The Lutheran Confessions are not to be enshrined on some altar as an object of reverence and worship. Everything written in the Lutheran Confessions was directed toward the practical administration and daily work of the Church. As the Lutheran confessors wrote, "We desire such harmony as will not violate God's honor, that will not detract anything from the divine truth of the Holy Gospel, that will not give place to the smallest error but will lead the poor sinner to true and sincere repentance, raise him up through faith, strengthen him in his new obedience, and thus justify and save him forever through the sole merit of Christ. . . ."[15]

Luther was very clear that the Church's practice must neither subtract from nor add to God's standards: "The most common and, at the same time, the most noxious plague in the churches is that people change what God has ordered, or that they grant preference to something else."[16]

CONFESSIONAL ECUMENISM

It is not enough simply to deplore the ecclesiastical divisions and fragmentation of the Church. Lutherans need to recognize the essential doctrinal dimension to such divisions. They must understand the causes of such division in the light of the nature and mission of the Church.

True Lutheran ecumenism is always confessional ecumenism. This means that Lutherans should approach their relationships with other Lutherans and Christians by means of attitudes, principles, and activities that are based upon the doctrinal content of the Lutheran Confessions as the true exposition of the Word of God. Much of the contemporary concern with ecumenical unity seems grounded on the secular mentality of "bigger is better." Such concern with numbers and size, however, is doomed to failure because Christians are to work, not in the might of men and numbers, but in the power of God who works through weakness and the lowly.

Confessional ecumenism will be both evangelical and evangelistic, accepting and employing Holy Scripture as "the only judge, rule, and norm according to which all doctrine should and must be understood and judged as good or evil, right or wrong."[17] The proper basis of such Lutheran fellowship lies in agreement in doctrine, not in human ceremonies, and in the recognition that Christian practice is the application of doctrine to life. Considerations of truth must always take precedence over considerations of love, should these ever appear to be in conflict. Christian love is always dependent upon the truth of the gospel.

Some Lutherans, especially those holding a low view of Scripture, have become indifferent to doctrine in their pursuit of ecumenicity. The criticism of such tendencies is something that any Lutheran concerned with the renewal of his or her Church will do with increasing regularity.

RENEWAL AND CHRISTIAN LIVING

The majority of Lutherans need to learn afresh that worship is just the beginning of what God wants from them during a week. Hands that have been folded in prayer need to be opened for service and for living for Christ. Feet that have stood before the altar of Christ need to walk worthy of the vocation wherewith the believer has been called (Ephesians 4:1).

Lutherans often suffer from undisciplined spirituality on one hand and the neglect of authentic Biblical spirituality on the other. They have sometimes feared pietism to such an extent that they have failed to understand and practice the sanctified life in the obedience of faith. Holy and pure doctrine must be matched with holy living.

At this time when renewal is such an urgent need of the Lutheran Church, Lutheranism needs men and women who will pray two prayers. The first prayer: "Lord, renew Your Church." The second prayer: "Lord, begin with me!"

A DIRECTORY OF RENEWAL GROUPS AND PUBLICATIONS IN LUTHERAN CHURCHES

"The Lutheran Hour" and "This is the Life," sponsored by the International Lutheran Layman's League (affiliated with the Lutheran Church—Missouri Synod, St. Louis, Missouri).

Fellowship of Evangelical Lutheran Laity and Pastors
1200 69th Avenue North
Brooklyn Center, Minnesota 55430.

World Confessional Lutheran Association
P.O. Box 7186
Tacoma, Washington 98407.

Lutheran Evangelistic Movement
833 Second Avenue South
Minneapolis, Minnesota 55402.

International Lutheran Renewal Center
Box 13055
St. Paul, Minnesota 55113.

Stewardship Growth Center
1914 Wendmere Lane
Fort Wayne, Indiana 46825.

Church Growth Center
0389 County Road 12
Corunna, Indiana 46730.

Affirm Magazine
c/o Walter Memorial Lutheran Church
4040 W. Fond du Lac Avenue
Milwaukee, Wisconsin 53216.

REV. HOMER TRICULES

is pastor of an American Baptist church in Scotch Plains, New Jersey. He has served as president of American Baptist Churches of New Jersey and as editor of *The American Baptist Fellowship Newsletter.* Rev. Tricules holds degrees from Rutgers University (B.S.), New Brunswick Theological Seminary (M. Div.), and Farleigh Dickinson University (M.A.).

FOUR
American Baptist Churches in the U.S.A.
Homer Tricules

P ut two Baptists in a room together for an hour and the result is likely to be three opinions! That quip has some truth to it. Baptists do have a strong tendency to be fiercely independent. Over the years, that characteristic has proved to be both a strength and a weakness so far as the history of American Baptist Churches in the U.S.A. is concerned.

The individualism of Baptists has been constructive in many ways; it has helped produce a number of important contributions to American religious life. But individualism can also lead to trouble. In the case of American Baptists, such trouble has included frequent distrust of one another, divisiveness, and an occasional division of the Church.

A BRIEF HISTORY

The work of Baptists in the northern part of the United States prior to the twentieth century was largely in the hands of local churches. This was due largely to the Baptist belief in the autonomy of the local church. Slowly during the nineteenth century some Baptists in the North formed voluntary associations that helped to build churches and colleges and support missionary activity. But the Baptist stress on independence left little room for the establishment of a national coordinating body.

What eventually brought about the formation of the Northern Baptist Convention in 1907 was missions. In the view of many American Baptists, what helped to keep this fellowship together over the years—through periods of intense disagreement—was missions. But at the same time it should be noted that it was a disagreement over missions and related issues that also produced the Church's biggest split. All this must be explained in due course.

Through most of the nineteenth century, many Baptists in the North supported three organizations: the American Baptist Home Mission Society, what came to be known as the American Baptist Foreign Mission Society, and the American Baptist Publication Society. After 1870 Baptist women in the North organized home and foreign mission societies of their own.

The 1900s brought a prevailing optimism to America. Baptists were not excluded from this. Masses of immigrants were arriving, the continent's coasts were joined by rail, the Spanish-American War was over, and Baptists in the North began to think in more orderly terms about the work of the gospel. The prevailing mixture of competing independent mission societies seemed inadequate for the task. After years of effort on the part of individuals like Henry L. Morehouse, the Northern Baptist Convention was born in 1907 in Washington, D.C., exactly two centuries after the founding of the earliest Baptist Association in the nation. The new convention gave Baptists in the North a way of introducing a greater measure of order in the matter of raising money for the Baptist societies.

In 1950 the convention changed its name to the American Baptist Convention. A further restructuring and name change occurred in 1972 as the convention became the American Baptist Churches in the U.S.A. Policy in ABCUSA is now made by a general board of two hundred members who are elected representatives of their districts. Executives of national programs as well as executives of regional and large local units make up a national council that coordinates the business of the church. There are presently some 1.6 million American Baptists and approximately six thousand local churches affiliated with ABCUSA.

PAST TENSIONS

After the formation of the Northern Baptist Convention in 1907, the convention experienced several decades of strife over such matters as the independence of the local church, creedal statements, governmental polity in the newly-formed denomination, and voluntarism as opposed to a more central control. While Southern Baptists opted for stronger centralized control, Baptists in the North moved in the opposite direction, toward voluntarism.

During the years between 1920 and 1947, the convention suffered from several waves of conflict caused by serious doctrinal disagreement along with, no doubt, the ever-present danger of self-aggrandizement. The presence of liberal or modernist beliefs in some Baptist institutions and the response of conservatives made the Northern Baptist Convention one of several battlegrounds for the fundamentalist-modernist controversy in the 1920s. There is probably little point in reliving the specific details of those days, even though they still affect Baptist relations and work in the North.

In the view of many, American Baptist Churches in the U.S.A. would be a much larger and more influential body today had it not suffered through its own periods of civil war. But in the interest of fairness, it should also be noted that the fundamentalists sincerely believed that doctrinal weaknesses in the convention obliged faithful Baptists to speak and to act. They were committed to the inspiration and authority of the Scriptures, to belief in the virgin birth, the substitutionary blood atonement, the bodily resurrection, and the Second Coming of Christ. Preserving the integrity of the historic Christian faith meant defending the proper place of such beliefs in convention institutions.

Of course, the dispute between fundamentalists (and other conservatives who might have wished to avoid the fundamentalist label) and modernists was often as much a disagreement over doctrine as it was a question of attitudes. The first split occurred in May 1932 when a number of churches left the convention and formed the General Association of Regular Baptist Churches. While the number of churches that left at first was relatively small (something less than fifty), the GARBC was a fellowship to which other fundamentalist churches in the convention moved over the years. A decade later, the second split began. Those who remained in the convention divided once more over similar issues of doctrine and charges of liberalism. Finally, in 1947 a significantly larger number of churches withdrew to form the Conservative Baptist Association.[1] Between them, the CBA and the GARBC have something over fifteen hundred churches and about five hundred thousand members.

It is difficult to see how there can be any winners in such divisions. While present-day members of the American Baptist Churches in the U.S.A. may hold differing interpretations and evaluations of what happened in the past, it is clear that everyone suffered.

SIGNS OF RENEWAL

Evangelical renewal is assuming somewhat different forms in each mainline Church. This should not be surprising because of the Churches' different histories and ecclesiology. It would be a mistake to judge the *quality* of renewal in a denomination by the *quantity* of its renewal movements. Denominations such as the Episcopal Church and the United Presbyterian Church show an abundance of renewal organizations, while renewal in the Methodist Church is being led effectively by primarily one movement.

Compared with what is going on in some of the other mainline Churches, a somewhat uninformed outside observer might think that relatively little in the way of renewal is occurring among American Baptists. The one renewal organization in ABCUSA, the American Baptist Fellowship, might appear to be doing relatively little. It meets infrequently (normally at the convention's biannual national meeting) and its one publication, *The American Baptist Fellowship Newsletter,* has not appeared in a while. But appearances, especially to outsiders unfamiliar with the actual dynamics of a denomination, can be deceiving.

Just as Baptist individualism contributed to past troubles, so present-day renewal is often occurring along individualistic lines. All students of renewal agree that renewal must begin with the individual Christian and then spread to the local congregation. Renewal is always a grass-roots movement. People familiar with the American Baptist situation believe that renewal is taking place, even if there is not always the presence of some visible renewal organization.

The old religious modernism to which the fundamentalists objected gradually died out and was replaced by a variety of theological systems. To be sure, some of the new systems were just as much in conflict with the teaching of historic Christianity. While some of the other systems still were built on a low view of Biblical authority, they were sometimes held in ways that made it possible for adherents to preach the Good News of the gospel. The point is not that conservative American Baptists were content with any of this; rather, the changing theological scene required conservatives to dialogue with less conservative colleagues in different terms. Central to all this was the growing conviction among American Baptist evangelicals that they would remain within the denomination they loved and work to increase the evangelical influence within the Church.

Many American Baptist evangelicals were heartened by the development of their Church's polity into a better coordinated structure of representative government. They were encouraged to hear once again of Baptist distinctiveness—but without the biting attitudes that prevailed in earlier years. Gordon Schroeder and Allan Knight published through Judson Press *Six Studies on the New Life in Christ.* To this day, it enjoys a wide circulation and acceptance across the country in many different kinds of churches as converts are taught about living for Christ as genuine, born-again persons—and as American Baptists. If the book needs a tag at all, it might be called lovingly evangelical. Throughout the land, American Baptists were learning to talk to each other with courtesy, to listen with patient open ears, to respect, to cooperate, to trust, and to love one another. The strong sense of autonomy in the local church is still alive. But it now seems less of a threat to cooperation and effective ministry.

Obviously, theological differences still exist. The Roger Williams Fellowship is left of center theologically, while the American Baptist Fellowship is right of center. But neither fellowship excludes anyone who wishes to belong. Both are loyal American Baptist groups, faithful to the American Baptist family, cooperative in American Baptist missionary work, and supportive of American Baptist institutions. Moving the headquarters of the denomination to Valley Forge, Pennsylvania, was a move forward towards better relationships, cooperation, and efficiency as our societies and agencies came together under one roof. There is less cantankerousness, greater openness to listen to one another, fewer people shouting angry epithets at each other, and best of all, a new understanding of the one gospel with its two thrusts; evangelism to win the lost to Christ, and the necessity of ministering in the social arena.

American Baptists no longer shy away from their Baptist distinctives.[2] Part of the reason for this turn of events is that we stopped the drastically damaging fighting. Disagreements no longer had to lead inevitably to division. American Baptists could differ, debate, and argue—without dividing.

A number of loyal American Baptists helped give birth to the American Baptist Fellowship. The name itself is significant in that it demonstrates the intent that they are and intend to remain within the denominational family they love, even with its flaws. The American Baptist Fellowship stands for and represents the evangelical voice of the denomination without the hypercritical attitudes that formerly characterized some conservative actions.

Dr. Lawrence T. Slaght was the first editor of the *American Baptist Fellowship Newsletter.* Dr. Slaght was renowned for his scholarly historic knowledge, for his astute wisdom and insight, and for his ability to see beneath the surface in order to relate happenings to one another. As a leader of the new evangelical group, Dr. Slaght's voice carried great weight everywhere as he spoke on behalf of evangelical American Baptists through the newsletter. One of the best ways to judge the course of evangelical renewal in ABCUSA over the last twenty years or so is to read the record contained in the pages of this newsletter. During the 1960s, editorship of the newsletter was passed from Dr. Slaght to a new editor. When the second editor's work as a home missionary grew, he found it necessary to surrender the editor's position. Because no replacement was available, the American Baptist Fellowship lost its voice of publication.

Unfortunately, the American Baptist Fellowship became dormant except for regional activity and some regional publishing. No doubt, this constituted a setback of sorts in the cause of evangelical renewal. However, there were plans to reactivate and reorganize the ABF at a January 1987 meeting at Eastern Baptist College in St. David's, Pennsylvania. The ABF still exists. It has a treasury and a membership. Following the Eastern College reorganization, it will once again be active on a national scale.

WHAT IS NEEDED?

Without question, evangelical renewal among American Baptists could be and should be stronger than it presently is. At the same time, this is true with regard to each of the denominations discussed in this book. Evangelical renewal among American Baptists depends on the same factors as evangelical renewal in any Church.

The first need is that of a vision. Individual American Baptist clergy and laypeople need a clearer vision of what evangelical renewal can do for their Church and for its ministry both at home and abroad. Another need is that of education. American Baptists need to be better informed about the needs of their denomination along the line of renewal. An essential part of this information is better training in doctrine. Informed evangelicals reject the claim that doctrine divides while evangelism unites. Proper Biblical evangelism has to be doctrinally sound. American Baptist laypeople need to be grounded in the essentials of sound doctrine. Third, the work of evangelism must continue, not only to those outside of our churches but also to members of American Baptist churches who somehow may have failed to grasp the gospel message of the new birth. And finally, each American Baptist needs to grow spiritually in the things of God. And as they grow, they need to apply what they receive from their faith to the problems of contemporary society.

DR. RONALD NASH

holds degrees from Brown
University (M.A.) and
Syracuse University (Ph.D.).
Nash is professor of
philosophy and religion at
Western Kentucky University
and the author or editor of
close to twenty books
including: *Poverty and
Wealth, Liberation Theology,
Social Justice and the
Christian Church,
Evangelicals in America, The
Concept of God, Christianity
and the Hellenistic World,
The Word of God and the
Mind of Man* and others.

The Presbyterian Church
Ronald H. Nash

A merican evangelicalism owes much to Presbyterianism. The traditional Presbyterian emphasis upon the authority of Scripture and the importance of thinking systematically about the teaching of Scripture produced a long line of Presbyterian scholars who did much to shape evangelical theology. Conservative Presbyterians were in the front lines during many of the liberal assaults against the inspiration, integrity, and authority of Scripture that have been so common during the past century. The writings of conservative Presbyterian scholars in such fields as New Testament, Old Testament, theology, and apologetics left modern evangelicalism an important legacy still worth careful study.

Regrettably, American Presbyterianism has fallen on hard times. During the last twenty years, mainline Presbyterianism has lost more than one million members—more than 25 percent of its membership in the mid-1960s. There are a lot of dissatisfied Presbyterians these days. There would be even more save for the fact that so many of the disaffected simply withdrew from the United Presbyterian Church in the U.S.A. (northern) or the Presbyterian Church in the U.S. (southern). Such vital signs as membership and giving provide strong evidence that mainline Presbyterianism has become an institution in decline. In the view of many, the blame for this decline belongs squarely at the door of an increasingly liberal or radical leadership that is insensitive to the convictions of the grass roots.

In 1983, northern (the United Presbyterian Church in the U.S.A.) and southern (the Presbyterian Church in the U.S.) mainline Presbyterian denominations merged to form the Presbyterian Church (U.S.A.). While some denominational leaders hoped the merger would stop the bleeding—or at least help hide it—the loss of members continues. In 1985, the last year for which numbers are available, the Church lost 43,000 more members. Among American Protestant denominations, only the United Methodist Church lost more.

But the numerical decline is only the tip of the iceberg. According to Richard G. Hutcheson:

> Along with the numerical decline has come a high level of internal stress: polarization between grassroots lay people and denominational leadership, between clergy and laity; fragmentation, as many congregations, ignoring denominational programs, have selected their own local or parachurch mission concerns; financial crisis, as money once devoted to denominational programs has been redirected elsewhere. All of these factors have contributed to the disarray of a denomination clearly in a pattern of diminishing strength and influence.[1]

Ervin Duggan points to another set of problems within the Church. "Within this democratically organized denomination," he writes, "there are today some sharp attitudinal cleavages. Indeed, a vast ideological gulf separates the rank-and-file Presbyterians from their official spokesmen—a gulf that raises an intriguing question. Is the Presbyterian Church (U.S.A.) in fact arriving at its political positions democratically, or have activists of a certain stripe seized control of the church's decision-making machinery?"[2]

What Duggan has in mind is the repeated practice of denominational leaders to support radical left-wing causes that are clearly opposed by the vast majority of Presbyterian laypeople. Duggan continues:

> While hundreds organize and determine to resist the leftward drift of their denomination by working within the church . . . thousands of other members are simply defecting. The Presbyterian Church, of all the mainline Protestant denominations, has been losing members in recent years at the fastest rate. Since 1966, the bodies that

now comprise the church have lost more than one million members.[3]

"Already," Duggan concludes, "thousands of Presbyterians are snapping their pocket books firmly shut and edging toward the exits, suspecting that their church has political bats in its belfry."[4]

Since organized renewal movements always arise in response to some perceived need, it is easy to see what issues concern evangelical Presbyterians by studying the objectives of the various renewal organizations within the Presbyterian Church (U.S.A.).

Evangelical renewal within the Presbyterian Church began in the mid-1960s with the formation of two movements now known as Presbyterians United for Biblical Concerns and the Presbyterian Lay Committee. Both movements grew out of a recognition of the denomination's need for doctrinal renewal.

At the time of the 1958 merger that produced the United Presbyterian Church in the U.S.A., there were many signs of theological disagreement. But the united Church agreed, outwardly at least, to accept the Westminster Confession as its statement of doctrine. After the merger, however, a movement began to produce a new confession. While the major objective of the new confession was stated to be the replacement of the outmoded language of the Westminster Confession by a more modern statement of Presbyterian beliefs, many conservatives came to realize that the real purpose was to replace the clear orthodoxy of the Westminster Confession with language that would give theological liberals within the U.S.A. Church more room to maneuver.

The renewal movement now known as Presbyterians United for Biblical Concerns began in 1965 under the name Presbyterians United for a Biblical Confession. Its original goal was to strengthen the theological content of the proposed new confession that the denomination finally adopted in 1967. After its work with regard to the new confession was finished, the organization expanded the scope of its work to include the task of evangelical renewal within the U.S.A. Church.

Another renewal organization that also developed in response to a concern for doctrinal renewal was the Presbyterian

Lay Committee, also started in 1965. The PLC was organized because of a concern that the U.S.A. Church was giving less attention to "its primary mission of preaching and teaching the Gospel of Jesus Christ" and was instead giving too much emphasis "to social and political action."

Other renewal organizations came along in the years after 1970. Some were concerned that too little attention was being given to the essential task of evangelism. Presbyterians Pro-Life was founded to present an alternative to the unfortunate stand the Church adopted with regard to abortion. Charismatic concerns were represented by Presbyterian Renewal Ministries. Presbyterians for Democracy and Religious Freedom was organized to counter denominational leaders' frequent support for Marxist causes and left-wing dictatorships around the world. The Presbyterian Evangelical Coalition supports the renewal cause by helping to organize and mobilize evangelical action within the denomination.

Presbyterian renewal movements differ in emphasis and style. Some are concerned primarily with doctrinal renewal or evangelism or spiritual renewal, while others focus on single issues such as abortion, homosexuality, or denominational leaders' support for left-wing social and political causes. Others are concerned with a broader sweep of issues.

The Book of Order of the Presbyterian Church (U.S.A.) provides for the existence of what are called "Chapter 9 Organizations." In the words of *The Book of Order,* "Members of a particular church or particular churches may associate together to conduct special tasks of witness, service, nurture, or other appropriate endeavors. . . . Where they cover territory larger than a synod, they shall be responsible to the General Assembly." Not surprisingly, a number of special interest groups within the Presbyterian Church (U.S.A.) have taken advantage of this opportunity. A number of the Chapter 9 Organizations represent evangelical concerns. Like all Chapter 9 Organizations, they make annual reports to the General Assembly and are expected to operate within guidelines set forth by the General Assembly.

The rest of this chapter will focus on four evangelical renewal organizations: The Covenant Fellowship of Presbyterians, The Presbyterian Lay Committee, Presbyterians for Democracy and Religious Freedom, and Presbyterians United for

Biblical Concerns. By all accounts, these are the largest and most active renewal groups. A study of their goals and methods is the best way to obtain a picture of the diverse concerns and styles of the renewal movements within the Presbyterian Church (U.S.A.).

THE COVENANT FELLOWSHIP OF PRESBYTERIANS

The Covenant Fellowship started in 1969 as a ministry to young people in the Presbyterian Church in the U.S. As its literature explains, the Fellowship seeks to serve the new united Church "by committing ourselves to maintain and promote a reformed and evangelical fellowship within the Presbyterian Church (U.S.A.) . . . [and] by praying and working for renewal throughout our denomination, especially at the local church level."

It is clear that the first task for this largely lay movement is evangelism. Its other objectives include helping Christians to grow in their commitment to Christ and to share their faith with others. The Fellowship pursues these goals by means of workshops, retreats for church officers, and lay renewal conferences. It continues to carry on a major ministry to Presbyterian young people through several large youth conferences.

The Covenant Fellowship publishes a bimonthly newsletter, *The Open Letter,* that presents an evangelical perspective on matters that concern Presbyterians. It is presently developing a ministry to women. The Fellowship's interest in world missions is expressed through local and regional missions conferences; it is active on behalf of a more aggressive mission program within the denomination.

THE PRESBYTERIAN LAY COMMITTEE

Headquartered in a suburb of Philadelphia, the Presbyterian Lay Committee expresses its opposition to the leftward drift of the denominational leadership in a monthly newsletter, *The Presbyterian Layman,* that is sent to over five hundred thousand readers.

According to its literature, the PLC and its supporters are concerned with what it sees as "wrong emphases in the church and the resultant losses in membership each year since 1966." Members of any denomination ought to be concerned about a loss of more than one million members; in this case, the total of lost members exceeds 26 percent. The PLC is also concerned about "the monumental reduction of the church's missionary force which at one time was one of the largest in the world." The PLC urges increased attention to "the need for an all-out reemphasis of evangelism by the church" that would make evangelism "the center of the church's activities."

The Committee is critical of the continuing failure "to appoint conservative-evangelicals as members of the church's agencies and boards." It deplores the extent to which the denomination's educational materials fail to be faithful to God's Word and to Reformed theology. It objects to "continuing support, by some, of the Consultation on Church Union (COCU) that would merge the major denominations into one super-church with the abolition of the rights of congregations and the office of elder." It criticizes the participation of the Presbyterian Church "in the World Council of Churches and that body's support of socialistic ideology and revolutionary groups." It also objects to Presbyterian "participation in the National Council of Churches and that body's support of radical, social-political-economic programs."

The literature of the Presbyterian Lay Committee draws attention to the movement's five major objectives:

1. To put greater emphasis on the teaching of the Bible as the authoritative Word of God in our seminaries and churches.

2. To emphasize at every opportunity the need for presenting Jesus Christ the Redeemer through preaching, teaching, and witnessing with evangelical zeal, as the primary mission of the church and to stress the need for regular Bible study and prayer.

3. To encourage individual Presbyterians to take their place in society and, as led by the Holy Spirit, to become involved in social, economic and politial affairs and to assert their position publicly as Christian citizens.

4. To encourage church bodies to seek and express the mind of God as revealed in Scripture on individual and corporate moral and spiritual matters. We therefore urge that official church bodies refrain from issuing pronouncements or taking actions unless the authority to

speak and act is clearly biblical, the competence of the church body has been established and all viewpoints have been thoroughly considered.

5. To provide an adequate and reliable source of information on significant issues confronting the church, including those being proposed for consideration at General Assembly or other governing bodies to enable Presbyterians to express an informed position.

While it is hard to see how any evangelical could differ with these objectives, a number of Presbyterian evangelicals prefer the style and methods of other renewal groups to the PLC. In the view of some, PLC tends to be too confrontational in its approach. PLC supporters answer such criticism by pointing out that serious errors call for strong words and action. In spite of occasional criticism, PLC supporters believe that "The Presbyterian Lay Committee . . . has become the rallying point for both lay people and clergy who believe in its objectives and who earnestly desire the strengthening of the Presbyterian Church. Many testify that the evangelical voice of the PLC encourages them to stay in the Presbyterian Church."

PRESBYTERIANS FOR DEMOCRACY AND RELIGIOUS FREEDOM

Presbyterians for Democracy and Religious Freedom, the youngest evangelical organization in the Presbyterian Church (U.S.A.), speaks for the growing number of Presbyterians who are disturbed by the radical, left-wing stance many denominational leaders and clergy exhibit on such issues as national defense and support for left-wing dictatorships. In the case of support for Marxist regimes in Cuba, Nicaragua, and other countries, Presbyterian radicals are in fact aiding nations that oppose political and religious freedom; in fact, some of these nations are actively engaged in persecuting Christians.

Even though Presbyterian church government is a form of representative democracy, it is becoming increasingly clear that the radical political positions that denominational leaders present as the views of the whole Church are not arrived at by any democratic process. According to The Presbyterian Panel, an ongoing opinion survey that the denomination itself commissioned, "rank-and-file church members tend overwhelmingly to be conservative-to-moderate in their approach to political and social issues. In a poll of April 1984, for example, 82 percent of lay Presbyterians and 86 percent of elders identified themselves as moderate or conservatives. Fewer than 2 percent identified themselves as 'very liberal.' "⁵ While Presbyterian pastors tend to be somewhat more liberal on such issues than their parishioners, the individuals who staff the boards, agencies, and offices of the denomination are substantially more liberal or radical than the grass roots. In the words of Ervin Duggan:

> Perhaps because these denominational staff members have more time and energy to devote to political issues than parish clergy or lay church members, it is *their* political attitudes and preferences that dominate virtually every official pronouncement of the Presbyterian Church (U.S.A.). And increasingly, these statements . . . reflect a set of political positions generally associated with the political left.⁶

Evangelicals regard support at the denominational level for Marxist dictatorships as "symptomatic of a markedly one-sided Presbyterian approach to issues of human rights and foreign policy."⁷

> Christian believers are enjoined in the words of the Book of Common Prayer, to "make no peace with Oppression." . . . The Presbyterian Church, through its official support for the Sandinista party in Nicaragua, through its implication that Marxist-Leninist revolutions in Central America somehow amount to "a conversion experience," and through its apparent acquiescence to Soviet religious repression, is failing that test. The official human rights positions of the church, shaped disproportionately by left-leaning . . . activists, are now demonstrably one-sided: indignant about tyrannies of the right, indifferent to tyrannies of the left, quick to condemn the United States as the source of most conflict and injustice in the world, largely silent about the foreign, military, and human rights policies of the Soviet bloc.⁸

According to the literature of the organization, the official position of PDRF is that totalitarianism of the Right or the Left is equally reprehensible. "Totalitarianism of the Left or the Right makes total demands on the individual's life and conscience that should be reserved for our ultimate sovereign: Christ Jesus. Totalitarianism is therefore a form of idolatry and a principal worldly foe of Christianity and democracy. The primary exponents of totalitarianism today are movements and governments shaped by the ideology of Marxism-Leninism, or Communism." For reasons like these, PDRF concludes: "Church agencies and representatives should offer no support—financial, organizational, or moral—to movements or apologists for totalitarianism in any form."

Presbyterians for Democracy and Religious Freedom has most recently set its sights on a booklet, *Presbyterians and Peacemaking: Are We Now Called To Resistance?*,[9] which is part of the denomination's Advisory Council's effort "to explore and recommend directions and policy" to the denomination's General Assembly on "such matters as the usefulness of traditional just war criteria in the nuclear age; witholding of taxes as an expression of resistance to military policy . . . non-compliance with selective service . . . and vocational withdrawal."

In the eyes of many Presbyterians, the booklet is a propaganda statement that expresses only one side of a highly complex issue and that calls for Presbyterians to become involved in highly questionable activities, including illegal actions against their government. Presbyterians for Democracy and Religious Freedom has published a book of its own that serves as its response to the denominational booklet. The PDRF book, *Peace-making? or Resistance?*,[10] contains essays by an impressive collection of Presbyterian laymen. The publication of the book appears to mark a new stage in evangelical determination to speak out on important issues in the Presbyterian Church.

PRESBYTERIANS UNITED FOR BIBLICAL CONCERNS

Presbyterians United for Biblical Concerns began in 1966 as an effort to mobilize conservative Presbyterians with regard to the writing of the new Presbyterian Confession that the U.S.A. Church finally adopted in 1967. PUBC was concerned with the neoorthodox view of Scripture and theological laxness scattered throughout the new confession. The goal of PUBC was to strengthen the theological content of the confession. After its work related to the new confession was finished, the organization expanded the scope of its work to include the task of evangelical renewal within the United Presbyterian Church, U.S.A. It now continues that task in the newly-merged denomination.

PUBC literature describes the organization in the following way:

> We are a fellowship of Presbyterians who love Christ and seek the spiritual revitalization of the Presbyterian Church. We are a theologically-oriented group of pastors and lay persons, best identified as evangelical, who understand the value of active involvement, and where necessary, creative dissent within the denomination. We desire to further the renewing work of the Spirit in obedience to the authority of God.

PUBC aims "to be a catalytic agent of reconciliation, reformation, and renewal" within the Presbyterian Church (U.S.A.). It seeks "to promote a definitive evangelical position through dialogue in a spirit of humility and good will . . . [and desires] 'to speak the truth in love,' while calling for Biblical integrity and accountability." In the words of Matthew Welde, executive director of PUBC, "We try to be bridge builders between evangelicals who feel alienated and estranged from the system and the denominational leadership." Welde explains, "This involves communication on both ends, letting leaders know what the evangelicals think and letting the people know when good things are happening up top." According to Welde, PUBC tries "to interpret for the leadership, much as an interpreter might, the concerns of grassroots, rank-and-file Presbyterians. We try to be a voice for people who feel somewhat disenfranchised. Another thing we can do is restore hope throughout the church. We say in a word, 'Hang in there. Don't despair. Things are bad, but there is an evangelical movement. The tide is coming in.' "[11]

PUBC is grounded on the conviction that Scripture is "the only infallible rule of faith and practice." It is committed to the full deity and humanity of Jesus Christ. Its supporters believe that human beings are lost because of sin and hence need salvation. They confess that human redemption is grounded only on the atoning death and resurrection of Jesus Christ; salvation comes by faith alone through the work of the Holy Spirit. PUBC stresses the importance of the Holy Spirit in equipping and enabling the Body of Christ to do the work of God. And it affirms its commitment to "a comprehensive and holistic mission of personal evangelism and social justice worldwide." It works to equip others for the work of Church revitalization.

The literature of the organization makes clear its commitment to spiritual renewal. Spiritual renewal begins as individual men and women are brought into a personal saving relationship with Christ. But spiritual renewal does not end with conversion. It also involves strengthening the entire Church to do God's work. Properly done, spiritual renewal will help the Church gain new life and strength through prayer, the study of God's Word, and Christian fellowship. Spiritual renewal also involves challenging Christians to live their lives in obedience to the Lordship of Christ.

But spiritual renewal cannot and should not be separated from theological renewal. Recognizing this, PUBC wants to stimulate theological dialogue with denominational leaders that will draw the Church's attention to the truth God has revealed in His Word. Along this same line, PUBC recognizes the importance of trying to influence denominational seminaries. It encourages a greater theological balance in the seminaries that will allow an evangelical voice to be available as future leaders of the Church prepare for the ministry. The organization also supports a referral service that helps evangelical pastors and pastoral search committees find each other.

The work of PUBC is aided by the publication of a quarterly magazine, *The Presbyterian Communique,* that is sent to twenty thousand homes. PUBC staffs an evangelical resource center at each General Assembly; the center makes position statements and background information on significant issues available to commissioners of the General Assembly. It also provides leaders who speak at hearings. PUBC speakers are also available to visit local churches to interpret actions of the General Assembly. Along with the Covenant Fellowship of Presbyterians, PUBC cosponsors an annual breakfast at General Assembly that features speakers who address central issues facing the Church. It seeks a greater balance on the boards, agencies, councils, and committees of the General Assembly by suggesting names of responsible evangelicals.

PUBC is active in other ways, as well. It holds national and regional conferences that provide information about significant Church issues; these conferences also aim to provide inspiration and personal renewal. In January 1985, PUBC joined with other Presbyterian renewal groups as a sponsor of the Dallas, Texas Presbyterian Congress on renewal; five thousand people attended.

PUBC also sees Christian missions as a dimension of its work. In 1976, it helped rebuild thirty-three Guatemalan Presbyterian churches that had been destroyed by the devastating earthquake that occurred that year. PUBC also has a role to play with regard to Church unity. It offers to act "as an agent of advocacy and reconciliation of persons and groups within the denomination and those who feel disenfranchised or alienated from it."[12] This includes dialoguing with dissatisfied evangelical churches that are considering withdrawal from the denomination.

It should be clear by now that PUBC differs from the Presbyterian Lay Committee and Presbyterians for Democracy and Religious Freedom by its less confrontational style. But it is also clear that all of the evangelical renewal movements within the Presbyterian Church (U.S.A.) have important roles to play and significant constituencies to serve.

CONCLUSION

Obviously, one might wish that mainline Presbyterianism did not need movements of evangelical renewal. But given the denomination's problems and its continuing decline, there is still reason to hope that those Presbyterian evangelicals who have thus far refused to withdraw will be able to have their voices heard and their views respected.

A DIRECTORY OF RENEWAL GROUPS AND PUBLICATIONS IN THE PRESBYTERIAN CHURCH (U.S.A.)

Association of Presbyterians in Cross-cultural Mission
51 Melrose Avenue
Albany, New York 12203

Seeks to encourage, promote, and provide a forum for discussion of a spiritual, holistic, and contemporary vision for global mission in the Presbyterian Church (U.S.A.)

Covenant Fellowship of Presbyterians
P.O. Box 8307 or 412 Uptain Building
Chattanooga, Tennessee 37411
The primary purpose is to promote a Reformed and evangelical fellowship working for the renewal of the denomination. This group, which is primarily programmatic in nature, provides services and resources while maintaining a national conference ministry, to youth, pastors of small churches, and other areas of need.

Literacy and Evangelism
1800 South Jackson
Tulsa, Oklahoma 74107
Conducts missionary work, both stateside and overseas, in the areas of adult literacy, evangelism, and lay witnessing.

The Outreach Foundation
P.O. Box 221095
Charlotte, North Carolina 28222
Supplements official cross-cultural missions by soliciting funds for evangelical missionary projects in the United States and overseas primarily in evangelism, new church development, and construction of new buildings.

Presbyterians for Biblical Sexuality
5742 Hamilton Avenue
Cincinnati, Ohio 45224
Encourages a Biblical approach to human sexuality by promoting family life and educating Presbyterians of Christ's healing power for homosexuals and other persons who desire healing of their sexual brokenness and sinful behavior.

Presbyterians for Democracy and Religious Freedom
20th Floor, First American Center
Nashville, Tennessee 37238-0106
Supports principles of freedom and democracy based on the nature of the Church which permits church members

to hear and obey the Word of God in their personal lives. The primary aim of PDRF is to offer Presbyterians a conservative view on social, political, and justice issues in contrast to the more liberal political views of the denomination.

Presbyterian Elders in Prayer
9500 Wornall Road
Kansas City, Missouri 64114
Encourages and mobilizes elders in the church to make a commitment to pray daily for renewal and growth of the denomination.

The Presbyterian Evangelical Coalition
1605 Elizabeth Street
Pasadena, California 91104
This group provides mutual encouragement, nurture, and fellowship for evangelical renewal organizations in the Presbyterian Church (U.S.A.). This group mobilizes united evangelical support on crucial issues where there is broad support by rank-and-file evangelicals.

Presbyterian Frontier Fellowship
6146 North Kerby Avenue
Portland, Oregon 97217
Promotes frontier evangelism to the hidden people groups which have no indigenous corporate witness within their culture or linguistic sphere. Both congregations and individuals are invited to contribute through "extra commitment giving" beyond the regular budget with accreditation by the denomination.

The Presbyterian Lay Committee, Inc.
1245 North Providence Road
Media, Pennsylvania 19063
Voices conservative opposition to the denomination's leftward drift by publication of a monthly newsletter, *The Presbyterian Layman* (mailed to over 500,000), lay chapters, and local church network to propose alternative perspectives/strategies on important issues.

Presbyterians Pro-Life
Research, Education, and Care, Inc.
P.O. Box 2153
Decatur, Georgia 30031
Promotes sanctity of human life from moment of conception through every stage of development until natural death. Offers responsible alternative to Church's prochoice stance.

Presbyterian Renewal Ministries
2245 N.W. 39th Street
Oklahoma City, Oklahoma 73112
Promotes spiritual renewal within a charismatic context, encouraging Presbyterians to claim the power of Pentecost through praise, prayer, edification, and fellowship.

Presbyterians United for Biblical Concerns
R.D. 4
Pottstown, Pennsylvania 19464
PUBC is a theologically-oriented fellowship promoting personal spiritual renewal, Biblical/theological renewal, ecclesiastical renewal in both the local and national church, and evangelism and mission renewal in the United States and overseas.

Presbyterians United for Mission Advance of Northern California
2407 Dana Street
Berkeley, California 94704
Engages about fifty churches in San Francisco Bay area in simultaneous missionary conference annually, and further promotes overseas and home interest in cross-cultural missions through a variety of educational and inspirational events in the local church.

United Presbyterian Center for Mission Studies
Presbyterian Center for Mission Studies
1605 Elizabeth Street
Pasadena, California 91104
Primarily a think-tank organization for Christian missions, PCMS gathers and disseminates available information con-

cerning cross-cultural Presbyterian and non-Presbyterian agencies which receive funds from members and congregations in the denominations.

United Presbyterian Order for World Evangelization
1605 Elizabeth Street
Pasadena, California 91104
Two-fold purpose of POWE is to promote frontier evangelization to those who remain outside the active evangelistic effort of any Christian organization and, further, to cultivate a modest life-style strengthened by a mutual covenant and a shared financial discipline. Assists churches in providing supplementary funding for "cross-cultural missions" over and above channels of denominational giving.

RENEWAL PUBLICATIONS IN THE PRESBYTERIAN CHURCH (U.S.A.)

Covenant Fellowship of
  Presbyterians
The Open Letter
(5 times per year)
412 Uptain Building
(P.O. Box 8307)
Chattanooga, Tennessee
37411

Literacy and Evangelism
  International
(newsletter, updates
periodically)
1800 S. Jackson
Tulsa, Oklahoma 74107

Presbyterian Elders in Prayer
(prayer newsletter
periodically)
9500 Wornall Road
Kansas City, Missouri 64114

Presbyterian Frontier
  Fellowship
Global Prayer Digest
(monthly)
Mission Frontiers
(12 times per year)
Center for World Mission
1605 Elizabeth Street
Pasadena, California 91104

The Presbyterian Lay
  Committee, Inc.
The Presbyterian Layman
(6 times per year)
1245 N. Providence Rd.
Media, Pennsylvania 19063

Presbyterians Pro-Life
Presbyterians Pro-Life News
(quarterly)
Research, Education and
Care, Inc.
P.O. Box 2153
Decatur, Georgia 30031

The Presbyterian Renewal
  Ministries
Renewal News
(6 times per year)
2245 NW 39th St.
Oklahoma City, Oklahoma
73112

Presbyterians United for
  Biblical Concerns

Presbyterian Communique
(4 times per year)
RD 4
Pottstown, Pennsylvania
19464

Presbyterians United for
  Mission Advance of
  Northern California
PUMA Pulse
(4 times per year)
2407 Dana St.
Berkeley, California 94704

GRANT EDWARDS

is editor of *Paraclete Journal,*
the quarterly publication of
The Conference on Spiritual
Renewal which is a
consortium of some four
hundred churches working
for renewal in the Disciples
of Christ, the Churches of
Christ, and the Christian
Church. Edwards is a
graduate of Cincinnati Bible
College and is a candidate
for a Master's degree at
Cincinnati Christian
Seminary. He has published
articles in *Good News, The
Lutheran Journal,* and
Restoration Quarterly.

SIX

The Disciples of Christ
Grant Edwards

T he Christian Church (Disciples of Christ) is part of what is known as the Restoration Movement. Even though the Restoration Movement began originally as an effort to unite all Christians, it eventually split into three separate movements: the Christian Church (Disciples of Christ), the Church of Christ (noninstrumental), and the Christian Church (instrumental). The last two movements are distinguished by the Church of Christ's conviction that no musical instruments should be used in the worship assembly. All worship singing is *a cappella*.

A proper understanding of these branches of the Restoration Movement and the current status of evangelical renewal within the Disciples of Christ is impossible without some understanding of the history of the Restoration Movement. The Restoration Movement, as it came to be called, was itself a synthesis of two separate frontier movements in the early 1800s. One of these movements was associated with Barton Warren Stone in Kentucky and the other with Thomas and Alexander Campbell in Pennsylvania.

THE CANE RIDGE REVIVAL

One of the most unusual revival meetings in the history of the Church occurred in 1801 at Cane Ridge, Kentucky. The pastor of a local Presbyterian church, Barton W. Stone, called a revival meeting at his church in early August. His prayers must have been answered since more than twenty thousand people eventually showed up.

The Second Great Awakening swept revival through the frontier in the early 1800s. The Cane Ridge Revival, the largest meeting of the Awakening, challenged a population that was becoming increasingly unconcerned about spiritual things. The thousands of people living there taxed the resources of the frontier area. Hundreds of horses, wagons, and people of all cultural and religious persuasions arrived to form a vast unorganized campground. It was a large open-air meeting with Presbyterian, Methodist, and Baptist ministers preaching simultaneously over an extended area.

While thousands were undoubtedly converted, there were many examples of religious frenzy. People fell to the ground where they remained apparently lifeless for hours. Others jerked uncontrollably, while still others ran laughing into the woods. While B. W. Stone found some of the scenes disturbing, he was more impressed by the fact that ministers of several different denominations had forgotten their differences to work together in a spirit of Christian unity.

The excesses as well as the doctrine being preached at Cane Ridge brought swift reaction in the Presbyterian Synod of Kentucky. The instances of religious frenzy offended the decorum of the Presbyterians, who were also offended by what they regarded as the "anti-Calvinistic" flavor of the preaching. Shortly Stone and four other ministers withdrew from the Synod of Kentucky and formed their own Springfield Presbytery.

On June 28, 1804, the Springfield Presbytery dissolved itself at the same time that it issued a document expressing opposition to the sectarian and divisive nature of creeds. The document also declared that the Bible was the only sure guide to heaven. It contained a call for Christian unity.

After the Springfield Presbytery dissolved, B. W. Stone used the impetus from the Cane Ridge Revival to build a movement that grew to three hundred congregations and fifteen thousand members by the year 1826. While Stone and his followers emphasized the need for freedom from divisive denominationalism, they eventually began to promote unity among all Christians. Stone firmly believed that only a united Church could accomplish the Church's mission of converting the world to Christ.

THOMAS AND ALEXANDER CAMPBELL

When Alexander Campbell was nineteen he had to be examined by the elders of the local Presbyterian Church in Glasgow,

Scotland, before he could participate in the semiannual Communion service. The presentation of a metal token following the examination signified that the Presbyterian Church considered Alexander doctrinally sound and thus qualified to participate in the Communion service that would follow. Grieved by the idea of the examination and the use of the token, Alexander returned the token, refused Communion, and in effect walked away from the denomination in which his father, Thomas Campbell, was a minister.

While Alexander was in Scotland, his father was in America, having arrived in 1807. After settling in Washington, Pennsylvania, Thomas waited for his family to follow him. While waiting, Thomas Campbell left the Presbyterian Church over a controversy that began when Thomas served Communion to some people who were not Presbyterians. When the Campbell family was finally reunited in America in 1809, both father and son found that they had walked similar roads in leaving the Presbyterian Church. Though separated by an ocean, both Thomas and Alexander Campbell had repudiated denominationalism.

After withdrawing from the Presbyterian Church, Thomas Campbell had become a free-lance minister who was free to serve Christians of any persuasion. In 1809, Thomas authored a document entitled *The Declaration and Address,* now viewed as the magna carta of the Restoration Movement. People within the Restoration Movement usually regard 1809 as the birth date of the movement. Thomas Campbell believed that Christian unity could be attained only as the Church abandoned creeds for the Bible alone. As Campbell wrote in the *Address,* "Nothing ought to be included upon Christians as articles of faith, nor required of them as terms of communion, but what is expressly taught . . . in the word of God."

THE UNION OF THE STONE-CAMPBELL MOVEMENT

The Campbells in Pennsylvania and the movement led by Stone in Kentucky united in the winter of 1831-32. Both Stone and the Campbells shared a desire for unity based upon the Bible; they also encouraged freedom of opinion. They shared a strong desire to reform the Church by restoring the practices of the New Testament Church. The key doctrines that came to characterize the Restoration Movement were the weekly observance of the Lord's Supper, baptism by immersion for salvation, and the independence of the local church. The Movement opposed creeds and denominationalism as divisive. The Movement adopted the motto, "Where the Scriptures speak, we speak; and where the Scriptures are silent, we are silent."

While Barton Stone was fifteen years older than Alexander Campbell, he recognized the younger Campbell's superior gifts and eventually yielded to Alexander as the leader of the movement. Alexander Campbell became the principal visionary, teacher, and leader of the Restoration Movement. While his father, Thomas, had started the movement in Pennsylvania and Stone had begun his movement in Kentucky, Alexander took their ideas, unified the two movements, and led the Restoration Movement during its formative years.

When the Stone-Campbell movements united in 1831-32, the people in the new fellowship numbered somewhere between twenty and thirty thousand. The Restoration movement grew rapidly to one hundred and eighteen thousand in 1850, to one hundred and ninety thousand in 1860, to one million in 1900, and finally reached a peak of approximately four and a half million in the late 1950s. Presidents James Garfield and Lyndon Johnson came from churches in the Restoration Movement, and even Ronald Reagan was once a member of a Disciples' church in Hollywood. People in the Movement started a number of educational institutions including Hiram College, Butler University, Drake University, Texas Christian University, and David Lipscomb College. The Restoration Movement has become the largest and most influential religious movement of those originating in the United States.

DIVISION WITHIN THE RESTORATION MOVEMENT

Although a concern for Christian unity was an animating force in the formation of the Restoration Movement, it is ironic that the Movement itself divided into three branches: the Church of Christ (noninstrumental), the Christian Church (instrumental), and the Christian Church (Disciples of Christ). There was clearly a problem somewhere. Either there was something inherently divisive within the Restoration Movement, or the heirs of the founders violated the original plea for unity.

The divisions within the Restoration Movement began in earnest when those who would become part of The Church of Christ (noninstrumental) developed the theory that nothing could be practiced in the Church that was not explicitly mentioned in the New Testament. Their battle cry was based on a strict interpretation of the Movement's original motto: "Where the Scriptures are silent, we are silent." The Christian Church (instrumental) developed its own version of a sectarian creed by insisting that any Christian not following their understanding of the New Testament pattern of living was in error. The Disciples of Christ left the Bible completely as they chased after liberal theology, an attachment to ecumenical unity, and a commitment to a liberal social-political agenda.

THE CHURCH OF CHRIST (NONINSTRUMENTAL)

The Church of Christ (noninstrumental) exhibits a number of internal divisions. Though all its churches oppose the use of instrumental music in worship, various subgroups within the fellowship divide over a number of issues. Some oppose parachurch organizations or Sunday schools or Bible colleges, among other things. To add irony to the tragedy, the subgroups often treat their own pet criteria as exclusive tests of the one true New Testament Church. So far as the Church of Christ (noninstrumental) was concerned, things really came to a head in 1906 when David Lipscomb (founder of David Lipscomb College in Nashville, Tennessee) notified the Census Bureau that the noninstrumental churches should be considered a Church separate from the rest of the Restoration Churches. The stricter members who fellowshiped with Lipscomb's noninstrumental movement were suspicious of organs, mission societies, and other things not mentioned in the New Testament.

The original Restoration motto ("Where the Scriptures are silent, we are silent") became the root of a serious problem. The question of what to do with things not mentioned in the New Testament began to receive increased attention. While some assumed that silence meant mandatory abstinence, others believed silence implied freedom. For a while, the nonuse of an organ remained a matter of opinion in the Restoration Churches. But for some, it eventually became first a doctrine and finally a test of fellowship. In this way, the original Restoration plea was betrayed by an overzealous creedalization of what had begun as a matter of opinion.

Under the leadership of David Lipscomb in the South and Daniel Sommer in the North, those who could not allow for things not mentioned in the Scriptures withdrew from those who could. The situation grew to the point where even D. Austin Sommer, Daniel Sommer's son, disfellowshiped his father over a point of Scriptural silence.

THE CHRISTIAN CHURCH (INSTRUMENTAL)

The next division within the Restoration Movement resulted in a split between the Christian Church (instrumental) and the Christian Church (Disciples of Christ). The conservative Christian Church withdrew from the Disciples over the issue of liberalism. Christians within the instrumental branch of the Restoration Movement began to realize the serious inroads that theological liberalism was making in their schools and institutions. Liberals were denying the inspiration and authority of the Bible along with essential doctrines of the Christian faith: the Trinity, the deity of Christ, the virgin birth, and the bodily resurrection of Christ.

The Disciples of Christ welcomed this kind of theological liberalism and pursued unity along ecumenical lines. While the more conservative Christian Church opposed such liberalism, it unfortunately withdrew into its own version of a narrow doctrinal sectarianism. A major element of the creedalism that came to characterize the Christian Church was the conviction that baptism by immersion was essential for salvation. This view of baptism became a test of fellowship as members of the Christian Church debated whether people baptized by some other mode than immersion or even whether people immersed in some other fellowship should be accepted as Christians. While the Disciples began to downplay baptism for the sake of unity, the Christian Church (instrumental) exaggerated their view of baptism at the expense of unity.

As liberalism spread through the Restoration Movement, it pervaded seminaries, conventions, and missionary agencies. The conservative Christian Church responded by forming new institutions. For example, the Christian Church began a system of

Bible colleges; of the forty-five colleges now affiliated with the Christian Church, probably forty-one were founded in reaction to the spreading liberalism. The conservative churches also formed the North American Christian Convention to counter the growing influence of liberalism in other conventions. Some historians use 1950, the year the North American Christian Convention became an annual event, to date the split between the Christian Church and the Disciples.

THE DISCIPLES OF CHRIST

The Disciples of Christ is now thoroughly liberal. Liberalism is no longer a debatable issue within the denominational hierarchy or its seminaries; it is simply assumed that everyone is liberal. As one history of the Disciples describes this liberalism:

> The genius of liberal theology was its openness to all truth and its insistence on genuine dialogue between church and world. Fearing nothing more than an outmoded faith, liberals reconstructed Christian theology in order to harmonize it with the prevailing currents in philosophy and science. . . . They defended the principles of biblical criticism on the ground that the Bible was not only the record of divine revelation but also an intensely human collection of documents.[1]

Liberalism crept into the Restoration Movement through the seminaries in which many of its future teachers and pastors were being trained. As late as the early 1900s there were still no first-class educational institutions within the Restoration Movement. Many from the Movement began to attend outside seminaries that were both highly academic and liberal in their teaching.

After earning a Ph.D. from the University of Chicago in 1896, H. L. Willett became dean of the Disciples' Divinity House, a cooperative educational effort between the University of Chicago and the Disciples. A prolific writer and speaker, Willett used this platform to crusade for liberalism within the Restoration Movement. Many historians give Willett credit for single-handedly popularizing the precepts of liberalism within the Movement. Willett explained his view of the inspiration and infallibility of the Bible by writing:

> Viewed from certain points of approach, it is unfortunate
> that the Bible has been called the Word of God . . . for
> even a casual reading of the documents that make up this
> unique collection shows that they were not written by
> God, nor even by men who were speaking with supernat-
> ural and inerrant knowledge of God's will. No error has
> ever resulted in greater discredit to the Scriptures or in-
> jury to Christianity than that of attributing to the Bible
> such a miraculous origin and nature as to make it an
> infallible standard of morals and religion.[2]

The liberal view initiated by H. L. Willett remains the
dominant position held by those who presently occupy positions of leadership in the Disciples. The infallibility of the Bible
is one option not permitted by the advocates of religious pluralism in the Disciples' branch of the Restoration Movement.
While some Disciples make allowance for "inspiration," they
define it in ways unacceptable to conservatives. When one
recent graduate of a Disciples' seminary asked his Old Testament professor if he believed in the inspiration of Scripture, the
professor replied by saying, "Yes, on the same level as Shake-
speare's being inspired while authoring his literature."

In 1968, the Disciples restructured itself from a loose association of churches into an organized denomination, thus becoming the Christian Church (Disciples of Christ). Under its
new organization, the denomination recognized a local, regional, and national-international Church with headquarters in Indianapolis, Indiana. A General Assembly (an assembly of local
church representatives) meets every two years to consider resolutions and a business agenda. Each resolution is presented to
the General Assembly by the General Board (a deliberative
group of two hundred fifty to three hundred that meets annually and is chosen by the General Assembly). The General
Board leans heavily to liberal theology and a liberal social-
political agenda. The General Assembly rarely turns down re-
quests from the General Board.

The 1968 restructuring represented a fundamental shift in
thinking for a previously antidenominational Restoration
Movement. The shift produced a significant response from the
grass roots. One year before restructure, the *1967 Year Book*
listed 8,049 Disciples churches. By 1970, this number had

fallen to 4,046. In just three years, the Disciples had lost 50 percent of its listed supporting churches. Many still on the list continued to support the reconstructed church only in a marginal way.

A primary reason for the restructure was to provide a platform from which the Disciples could work as equals with other denominations to further the goal of ecumenical unity. This quest for unity led many Disciples to resist suggestions that they were betraying the original principles of the Restoration Movement. While many Disciples believed they were furthering the Restoration Movement's goal of unity, some did express serious reservations about the 1968 restructuring of the Church. As W. A. Welsh wrote,

> The fear here may be expressed in a question: will restructure really serve to strengthen our "spirit" as a brotherhood, thereby making us more effective in evangelism? . . . [Another] fear is that restructure may mean the loss of our distinctive Disciples' witness—that is, that the results of restructure will be simply . . . the achievement of a cheap Christian unity, a sort of "unity-at-any-price" kind of procedure.[3]

RENEWAL IN THE CHRISTIAN CHURCH (DISCIPLES OF CHRIST)

In 1986, the Disciples experienced their twenty-second straight year of membership decline. Their numbers have dwindled from a peak of 2.2 million in 1964 to 1,121,301 in 1985.[4] During the 1985 calendar year, the Disciples lost forty-four members per day. Because the remaining number of members contains such a high percentage (estimated as high as 38 percent) of elderly people, it seems clear that the future continues to hold only bad news for the Disciples in this matter. Of the 4,251 churches listed in the current Disciples' *Yearbook and Directory*, only 177 have shown significant growth over the last five years. At the present rate of membership decline, the Disciples will simply cease to exist by the year 2027.

Some leaders look upon the losses as a pruning process that is eliminating churches and members not committed to the liberal social-political-theological agenda of the denomination. Others, not wanting to sound negative, hope the decline is nothing more than a temporary downswing. But the problems are not temporary. Much more than a pruning process has been taking place. To use a more apt analogy, the denomination has been doing its best to commit spiritual suicide.

Liberalism is without question a major culprit in the decline. According to Leroy Garrett, the Disciples' serious decline in membership "is due to a lack of spirituality in the pulpit even more than the pew. If the conservative churches are growing because of strong Bible-centered teaching and preaching, the Disciples, along with other liberal churches, are losing ground for a lack of it."[5] The greatest percentage by far of growing churches in the Disciples movement are conservative.

A second reason for the continuing decline of members in the Disciples movement is the growing polarization between the liberal denominational hierarchy and conservative pastors and laypeople. The denominational leadership lost contact with the grass roots long ago; its discrimination against conservative pastors and churches is easily seen. Some believe the growing frustration the grass roots feels with regard to the Church's leadership is reaching the crisis stage. As one pastor puts it,

> Some of us are deeply concerned about current trends in our denomination, and we have been relatively silent for too long. And like water building up behind a dam, the pressure may become too great to contain properly. . . . We are weary of sensing that we are "on the outside looking in." . . . It is our belief that most of the actions taken by the General Assemblies at the behest of the General Board and by some of our agencies and commissions are dictated by the most liberal portion of our brotherhood. It is our further opinion that many of these actions are taken without regard for the consequences on the total membership.[6]

In the words of another pastor,

> I do not feel that the bias against a conservative voice in my denomination is in any way subtle. I believe the bias against conservatives is very blatant and deliberate. There is no such thing as an evangelical Disciples of Christ seminary. Conservative ministers are discriminated against in the granting of degrees and in career opportunities and

advancement. The leadership at the top tends to be autocratic and hostile toward any democratic processes.

Moreover, there is a lack of evangelism and spiritual leadership in the Church. Donald McGavran is a Disciples minister, founding dean of the School of World Missions at Fuller Theological Seminary, and a leading authority on church growth. According to McGavran,

> The Christian Church (Disciples of Christ) is in urgent need of renewal. Like many other branches of the universal church, it has ground to a halt. . . . It could easily grow, but it does not. If it is to be renewed, it must recognize and incorporate the essential element in renewal—finding and holding the lost.[7]

Herbert Miller, executive director of the National Evangelistic Association, contends that leadership must also be developed. In his view,

> Methods alone are not enough! We currently have more than a dozen evangelism plans at our disposal. . . . What we seem to lack is the will to use these plans. . . . What produces motivation? Leadership! . . . Faith and courageous action are generated by leadership.[8]

The Disciples of Christ are at a crossroads. They will either undergo renewal or they will continue to shrink in size, influence, and effectiveness of ministry. Can the influence of liberalism be overcome? Can the disillusionment of conservative pastors and laypersons be eased? Can the vision of evangelism be restored? Fortunately, there are many individuals and groups striving for renewal within The Disciples of Christ. Such agents of renewal are calling the Disciples back to the historic positions of the Church: belief in the inspiration and authority of the Bible; in such essential doctrines of Christianity as the Trinity, the deity of Christ, His atonement for human sin, His bodily resurrection; and in Biblical evangelism.

RENEWAL GROUPS IN THE DISCIPLES OF CHRIST

One organization seeking renewal within the Disciples of Christ is the National Evangelistic Association of the Christian

Church (Disciples of Christ).[9] Although the NEA began as a grass-roots advocate of evangelism in 1904, it remained loosely organized and poorly funded until its reorganization in 1977. With a current annual budget of $500,000, the NEA has grown into a year-round research and development resource center. The NEA has one goal: to help churches and individuals fulfill the Great Commission of winning men and women to a deep and lasting commitment to Jesus Christ. The NEA is dedicated to increasing membership in the Disciples to two million by the year 2000. To reach this goal, the NEA produces dozens of evangelistic programs, sponsors conferences, and provides local congregations with consultation on church growth. NEA publications include *Net Results,* a magazine about evangelism and church growth.

Another renewal movement is the Conference on Spiritual Renewal, located in Nashville, Tennessee. Since its birth in 1980, the CSR has held an annual conference that has attracted more than three thousand registrants from over five hundred local churches. The members of the Steering Committee represent all three branches of the Restoration Movement, making CSR one of the few organizations with an active ministry to the entire Movement.

CSR believes God is using a renewed emphasis on worship, the implementation of spiritual gifts, evangelism, discipleship, prayer, and small groups to encourage renewal in the Church. The Conference on Spiritual Renewal publishes *Paraclete Journal* four times a year, as well as *Networking,* a monthly newsletter. In addition to its annual conference held in Nashville, the CSR puts on regional conferences throughout the country.

Another important renewal instrument is the magazine *Disciple Renewal.* The magazine was started by three Disciples pastors in 1985 who were concerned about the growing liberalism in their Church as well as the increasing number of evangelical Disciples who were withdrawing from the denominational assemblies. *Disciple Renewal* was created to inform and encourage conservative pastors and laypeople within the Disciples movement. As one of the founding pastors explains,

The real issue that brought *Disciple Renewal* into being is biblical authority. Disciple evangelicals hold many concerns in common, but our unifying factor is the belief that the Bible is the inspired Word of God and the believer's final authority in matters of faith and practice.[10]

Another publication worth noting is *Restoration Review,* edited by Dr. Leroy Garrett. Garrett, holder of a Ph.D. from Harvard and a former professor of philosophy at several colleges, comes from a Church of Christ (noninstrumental) background. His journal calls all heirs of the Restoration Movement to return to the original concerns of Barton W. Stone and Alexander Campbell. Because of Garrett's irenic spirit, the *Restoration Review* is read by members of all three branches.

A unique set of circumstances brought about the formation of the next renewal movement to be mentioned. As an example of structural union, the Disciples of Christ merged Disciples churches in India with the primarily Episcopal Church of North India. Twenty-two of the twenty-eight affected churches decided not to join the Church of North India. Through the Division of Overseas Ministry, the Disciples proceeded anyway and gave the Church of North India all mission property, including the properties of the churches that opposed the agreement. As Donald McGavran put it, the Disciples Church in America is using property "as a club to force all [of the Indian congregations] into the Episcopal Church."[11]

The Continuing Christian Churches Movement was started to support the churches in India that wish to remain part of the Disciples movement. CCCM now supports a group of churches in a similar situation in Great Britain. The purpose of CCCM is to provide a fellowship of local congregations within the Disciples who want to continue pioneering mission efforts and support missions abandoned by the Disciples Division of Overseas Ministries. CCCM publishes a free monthly newsletter.

The last renewal movement to be mentioned here is Christian Mission Awareness. CMA does not itself send missionaries but rather provides information to Christians about important mission trends and issues. The CMA seeks to inform Disciples of ways in which the denominational leadership is transforming "missions" from the traditional task of spreading the gospel to providing financial aid that often ends up in the hands of Marxist revolutionaries.

CONCLUSION

As other chapters in this book make clear, evangelical renewal takes several basic forms. Few denominations in America exhibit the need for theological renewal more than The Disciples of Christ. While the Church of Christ (instrumental) and the Christian Church (noninstrumental) have remained basically more faithful to the Restoration Movement's Biblical heritage, they along with the Disciples evidence plenty of need for the second type of evangelical renewal—i.e., spiritual renewal. The branches of the Restoration Movement need once again to give evangelism the priority it used to have in the Movement. Ironically, there is now an urgent need for evangelism among members of Restoration churches. Restoration pastors need personal spiritual renewal and need to give the Scriptures a central place in the life and worship of their churches. Without genuine evangelical renewal, all signs suggest that the decline of The Disciples will continue. Without evangelical renewal, the future may hold similar decline for the other two branches of the Restoration Movement.

A DIRECTORY OF RENEWAL GROUPS AND PUBLICATIONS IN THE RESTORATION MOVEMENT

The National Evangelistic Association of the Christian Church (Disciples of Christ), 5001 Avenue N., Lubbock, Texas 79412. Telephone: 806 762-8094. Publications of the NEA include the magazine *Net Results.*

The Conference on Spiritual Renewal, P.O. Box 40325, Nashville, Tennessee 37204. Telephone: 615 385-2905. One ministry of the Conference is publication of the quarterly magazine *Paraclete Journal,* 3707 Edgewood Drive, Cincinnati, Ohio 45211.

Disciple Renewal, P.O. Box 106, Lovington, Illinois 61937.

The Continuing Christian Churches Movement, 1720 W. Seventeenth St., Santa Ana, California 92706. Telephone: 714 547-4173. CCCM publishes a free monthly newsletter.

Restoration Review, 1201 Windsor Drive, Denton, Texas 76201.

Christian Mission Awareness, Inc., P.O. Drawer 1527, Grafton, Virginia 32692.

REV. GERALD SANDERS

is executive director of
Biblical Witness Fellowship,
an evangelical renewal
organization within the
United Church of Christ.
Rev. Sanders has ordained
ministerial standing in the
Western Association of
North Carolina, United
Church of Christ. Sanders
holds degrees from East
Tennessee State University
(B.S. and M.A. in
philosophy). He has also
studied at Duke Divinity
School. He is a candidate for
the D.Min. degree from
Lutheran Theological
Southern Seminary. In
addition to serving as editor
of *The Witness* and as
contributing editor to *Issues
in Sexual Ethics,* Rev.
Sanders has authored a
number of articles for
religious journals.

SEVEN
The United Church of Christ
Gerald M. Sanders

M any people believe that no denomination in the United
States has moved as far to the left as the United Church
of Christ. It has gone farther to adopt contemporary values in
sexual ethics, inclusive language, nonevangelical models of missions, and other trappings of radical left-wing theology than
any other mainline denomination. And yet there are numbers
of people within the United Church of Christ who believe the
UCC can be reformed and renewed. There are presently over
forty thousand such people who are contributing to and working for this renewal.

The United Church of Christ was the last major denomination in the United States to develop a grass-roots renewal movement. An adequate answer to why this was so must begin with
an understanding of the denomination's origins and polity.

The United Church of Christ is one of America's younger
denominations. It was formed in 1957 by the merger of the
Evangelical and Reformed Church and the Congregational
Christian Churches.

The Evangelical and Reformed Church was itself the result
of a merger between the Evangelical Synod of North America
and the Reformed Church in the United States. Both Church
traditions were German in background. At the time of their
merger, they adopted the Shorter Catechism of Luther and the
Heidelberg Catechism as adequate statements of their common
faith under, of course, the final judgment of Scripture. Their
polity was presbyterian in style with final authority resting in
regional synods.

The Congregational Christian denomination was made up
of a free association of Congregational Churches and Christian

Churches. This association had been formed in the late thirties because the Congregational Churches and Christian Churches viewed themselves one in purpose and in understanding regarding the content of the Christian faith. The Congregational Churches had their roots in English Reformed thought and first came to America during the settlement of Plymouth Colony. The Christian Churches had their origins in a group of dissatisfied Baptists in New England and in the O'Kelly movement within the Methodist Church in the late eighteenth century.

While the Congregational Christian Churches had, from time to time, issued "statements of faith" such as the Kansas City Statement, it had no formal set of doctrines which applied to the whole Church. While generally orthodox, it was not set in the same kind of confessional mold as the Evangelical and Reformed Church. Its polity was congregational. It gave final authority in all matters of local church practice to the local congregation. The support of activities beyond the local congregation was dependent upon a vote of the local congregations. The denomination did form various committees and boards for work beyond the local church. But congregations were not obliged to support the work of these groups, nor were these committees and boards obligated to follow the dictates of the local congregations if they had funds apart from those supplied by local congregations.

The merger between the Congregational Christian Churches and the Evangelical and Reformed Church was born out of the ecumenical optimism—some would say naiveté—of the 1930s. There were obvious differences between the polity of the two groups and even more profound differences in the theology of the partners in the merger.

The Congregational tradition understood the Church to exist only locally; all other aspects of the Church were free associations which had a life separate from the parts. The E & R tradition saw all local and denominational parts of the Church as aspects of the same organic union, with each being accountable to the other.

The Congregational tradition allowed local congregations to set their own criteria for membership in the congregation. The E & R, while tolerant, was clear on the content of the faith it affirmed, not just locally but all the way to the General

Synod. Although some in the E & R may not have personally accepted Luther's Shorter Catechism or the teachings of Heidelberg, these documents were clearly the public confessional teachings of the E & R Church.

At one point, Dr. Louis Gobbel, president of the E & R, insisted that the union would have to be organic and not merely a free association of the E & R and CC Churches for joint mission work and witness. Dr. Truman Douglas of the CC Churches assured Gobbel that this was his aim and understanding. A document called the Basis of Union was drafted by a joint committee of both denominations. While the document was adopted by the E & R Church, the Congregationalists at first refused because they felt it denied local autonomy. To end Congregational opposition, a list of "interpretations" was attached to the Basis of Union which affirmed local autonomy in all matters. Thus modified, the document was adopted by the Council of Congregational Christian Churches and sent to congregations for ratification. The E & R's, however, were thrown into consternation since they recognized that the "interpretations" compromised their position on organic unity. The Congregationalists gave assurances that this was not the case. After considerable debate, the E & R Church adopted the Basis of Union with the "interpretations."

The United Church of Christ came into being in 1957 with the adoption of this document by the E & R General Synod and a majority of local Congregational Churches. However, subsequent events have shown that the concerns of the late Dr. Gobbel were justified. Those concerns also, it turns out, dealt with issues that have caused many of the problems facing the United Church of Christ today.

The E & R entered the merger believing there would be an organic unity in the UCC. They assumed a continuation of the system of mutual accountability between local congregations and the General Synod. They felt that to differ with the General Synod or any of its leaders was to differ with the Church proper. This made it very difficult for them to register public objection to acts of the Synod or its officers. It also helps to explain why renewal and reform movements in the denomination were so slow to develop.

The Congregationalists understood the merger differently. In their view, the polity of the UCC was basically unchanged

from that of the Congregational Christian Churches. But the
E & R's traditional emphasis upon unity meant that the leadership of the new denomination could count on financial support
from the German congregations even when those old E & R
churches disagreed with their actions. This had the effect of
making UCC leaders and agencies less responsive to the feelings
of the grass roots. Many local congregations of the Congregational tradition who did object to actions by the denominational leadership continued to act as autonomous bodies; many left
the denomination. For such congregations, leaving the denomination was the only option to facing continued defeat at the
hands of a powerful political establishment which had and still
has control of the UCC.

What the UCC needed was something to wake the local
congregations from their slumber and provincialism. The denominational leadership itself provided the bombshell—at the
11th General Synod, which met in late June 1977 in Washington, D.C. It came in the form of a human sexuality report
prepared by the Board of Homeland Ministries and submitted
to the General Synod for adoption. This work was a careful
attempt to present views which differed radically from the
traditional and historic teaching of Christianity on a number of
issues, ranging from homosexuality to the doctrine of the Fa-
therhood of God. The sexuality report adopted the stance of
theological radicals who affirmed the viability of homosexuality and of sexual relationships outside marriage; it also rejected
the Church's traditional language about God as contained in
Scripture. The report failed to include any significant criticisms
of such views.

When the delegates gathered for the open meetings to
discuss the various pronouncements and resolutions, concerns
were expressed about the biased nature of the human sexuality
study. Barbara Weller, a laywoman, and Martin Duffy, a pastor,
both presented eloquent critiques of the study and challenged
its unfaithfulness to the teachings of Holy Scripture and the
historic teachings of the Church. While the report, *Human
Sexuality, a Preliminary Study*, was passed by the Synod, more
than a third of the Synod voted against it. Those voting in the
minority appealed to the UCC Constitution which grants any
minority view above 25 percent of the Synod the right to file a
minority report. The report was written and adopted by the

Synod, although limitations of time prevented a long and detailed report.

The majority report on human sexuality outraged people
across the denomination. Large numbers of people contacted
Mrs. Weller to express their support of the position she and the
minority had taken. A group supporting them met with the
president of the UCC, the heads of the United Church Board
for Homeland Ministries, and the head of the Office for
Church Life and Leadership in the New York offices of the
denomination. The group expressed its concern that a view
held by many in the Church was being ignored in denominational publications. Mrs. Weller and others in the group argued
that the small minority report published in the minutes of the
General Synod was inadequate to represent the full views of
UCC members opposed to the majority report. One member of
the group expressed concern that the majority report conflicted
with views held by most people in the UCC. He was told that
the Board of Homeland Ministries had never taken its directions from the churches and had no plans to do so in the
future. The meeting proved to be a major disappointment for
those seeking reconciliation within the Church.

The committee returned to Pennsylvania and voted to call
a Convocation on Human Sexuality to discuss the human sexuality report and determine what should be done to get the
minority view circulated among the local churches. This convocation was held in April 1978 at Old First Reformed Church in
Philadelphia. One thing that became clear there was that the
issue before the UCC was much larger and more important
than the problem of human sexuality. The real issue was the
question, What will be the ultimate authority for the faith and
practice of the United Church of Christ? Those who gathered
in Philadelphia believed that it was important to affirm God's
infallible Word as sole authority for the Church. Feeling the
need for the formation of an ongoing group to influence the
denomination at the national level, those present at the meeting
elected regional representatives. These representatives met following the meeting to organize and to choose a name, United
Church People for Biblical Witness.

Barbara Weller was elected president and began immediately to move the group towards witnessing on behalf of the
historic faith made known in the Holy Scriptures. The group

decided to publish a newsletter, *The Witness,* as well as a study book that would offer a counterpoint to the book produced by the Board of Homeland Ministry and adopted by the General Synod. UCPBW's book, *Issues in Sexual Ethics,* was mailed free of charge to every pastor in the United Church of Christ. It helped to generate significant support for the Biblical Witness movement. The newsletter, which had begun publication earlier, had already received a sympathetic hearing across the Church and brought contributions that provided a financial basis for the subsequent work of the Biblical Witness movement. Thanks in large measure to the early efforts of the movement, local congregations began to stir and to assume more responsibility for the direction of the denomination.

As the time for the 12th General Synod of the UCC drew closer, pastors and laypeople within the Church who were committed to the historic faith hoped that the Synod would mark a new beginning for the denomination. The human sexuality issue had produced considerable tension in the Church. Various resolutions expressing displeasure with the position taken by the 11th General Synod were sent to the secretary of the Church. People sympathetic to the position of the Biblical Witness movement believed that an open discussion of their resolutions at the General Synod would bring positive results.

When the 12th General Synod met in late June 1979, the UCPBW and its supporters learned how those in control of the UCC play the game of church politics. It proved to be a valuable lesson since it made the people working for change aware of what they were up against. It was a healthy thing to be cured of naiveté, for in a purely political situation such an affliction can be fatal.

All resolutions sent to the General Synod are first referred to committees made up of delegates chosen at random. The resolutions on human sexuality were referred to the Committee on Human Sexuality. While the UCPBW always had the support of at least 30 percent of the delegates to the Synod, the allegedly "random selection" of members to the committee that would consider the resolutions resulted in the selection of only two supporters of the UCPBW position. No other conclusion was possible: the deck had been stacked.

Prior to the meeting of the General Synod, the Executive Council of the United Church of Christ recommended that a task force be appointed to deal with all human sexuality issues and report back to the 12th General Synod. The president of the Church, Dr. Avery Post, was to appoint the task force. This recommendation was forwarded to the General Synod Committee on Human Sexuality.

When the Human Sexuality Committee met, it spent almost all of its time discussing the proposal from the Executive Council. In the closing minutes, it voted to establish the task force and then referred all the remaining proposals and resolutions from the churches to the task force. The effect of this action was to keep the resolutions sent by the churches away from the floor of the Synod and to put them in the hands of a task force that would be under the control of denominational officials from the start. When the task force was appointed, only one person from the UCPBW was appointed to it. After protests, President Post appointed another person; but the force still remained unrepresentative of the voting percentages of the past Synod.

Across the denomination, laypeople began to realize what some had known from the first. The General Synod and the leaders of the Church operate with a different concept of the Church. The E & R's saw that the concept of organic unity between the national offices and the local church did not exist.

In the years following the 12th General Synod, the UCC Synod and its leaders have affirmed increasingly radical positions on theology. As disturbing as this has been to more traditional members of the Church, the emergence of the UCPBW gave such people an alternative to withdrawal from the denomination.

The UCPBW Board of Directors decided to make one more push to get the issue of Scripture as authority for the faith and practice of the Church before the Synod. They planned to make this effort at the 1983 meeting of the Synod in Pittsburgh. Prior to the Synod, a Pronouncement on Christian Family Life was carefully drafted. While careful to show compassion and understanding for all persons, it asserted that the Holy Scriptures approve only two sexual lifestyles: heterosexual relationships within marriage or celibacy. This pronouncement had the support of many congregations throughout the UCC. There was little hope that the pronouncement would pass the Synod. The real aim was to force the Synod to say yes or no to the normative status of Scripture and to the Church's traditional understanding of its teaching on this important subject.

The ramifications of a vote on the resolution were clearly understood by the UCC leadership. In an effort to keep the issue from a vote, the Pronouncement was referred to the Synod Committee on Family Life, which then voted to refer it to the Board of Homeland Ministries Committee on Family Life. When the motion from the Synod Committee to refer the Pronouncement to the second committee came to the floor of the Synod, a delegate sympathetic to the UCPBW position moved to "substitute the original motion for the main motion." This meant that the Synod would have to say yes or no to the introduction of the original Pronouncement; it meant that the Synod would have to say yes or no to the issue of Biblical authority. It said no by refusing the original motion.

The Synod at Pittsburgh made it clear that the United Church of Christ could not be reformed or renewed from the top down because the leadership completely controlled the Synod. In fact, their control seemed to be growing stronger.[1]

The people who led the UCPBW loved the Church. They were unwilling to see it continue to lose members and see its mission-work for Jesus Christ fail. It was clear to them that the leadership of the denomination would continue to take positions that would alienate the membership of the Church. While radical action now seemed necessary, it had become obvious that the Synod level was not the place to begin that action. The Synod was becoming increasingly irrelevant to the life of the local churches.

During the meeting of the Pittsburgh Synod, there was much prayer over what action should be taken as things went from bad to worse in the life of the denomination. On the last day of the Synod, the UCPBW issued a statement entitled "A Call to a Confessing Fellowship." This statement argued that there were limits to the theological pluralism dominating the UCC establishment. It was time for those who believed that there are limits to what may legitimately be called Christianity to speak. The limits need to be defined for our time and confessed before the world; they need to be the basis of action in the life of the Church.

In November 1983 at Dubuque University in Iowa, the United Church People for Biblical Witness met for what would be their final meeting. They gathered to discuss the future of their work for renewal in the United Church of Christ. The Board noted that the response to their call for a confessing fellowship following the 1983 Synod had received wide support. They felt a mandate to respond to this call from the churches. Since their efforts at the Synod level had failed, they declared the need for a new organization that would minister at the grass-roots level and allow renewal and reform to flow upward to the top levels of the Church. The new association would require a new organization and a confessional basis. It would also need some full-time staff members to replace the volunteer workers who had led the UCPBW.

A new committee under the leadership of Pastor Martin Duffy, Dr. Donald Bloesch, Pastor Fred Poorbaugh, and others began the process of drafting a confessional statement. They agreed to call their work a "Declaration" since they did not believe a single group had the authority to write a confession of faith. What they intended was a declaration about the Christian faith in relation to contemporary issues in the life of the United Church of Christ. Following minor revisions of the Board of Directors, what would become known as The Dubuque Declaration was sent to supporters for ratification and subscription.[2]

The writers of The Declaration made a careful effort to remain faithful to the theological heritage of the United Church of Christ. Barbara Weller pointed out that the assertions in The Dubuque Declaration are not really new, but are instead a faithful restatement of valued theological assertions which had a role in the shaping of the United Church of Christ. Another leader of UCPBW stated that it was the leaders of the denomination who were giving human experience priority over Scripture, who were creating something new. It was the denominational leaders who were attempting to rewrite the faith of the UCC. This new faith of the denominational leaders, he declared, "is alien to the history of all four traditions involved in the UCC."

The Dubuque Declaration claims as its basis the faith affirmed in the Basis of Union and the Constitution of the United Church of Christ. Both documents set forth a clear and faithful statement of the orthodox Protestant faith. The six points that follow the preamble of the Declaration speak to separate threats to the faith of the United Church of Christ.

The first point declares: "We confess our faith in the triune God—Father, Son and Holy Spirit." This point addressed what Dr. Donald Bloesch called "a creeping Unitarianism" in the UCC. This trend has developed out of inclusive-language theology which merges the "Persons" of the Holy Trinity into nonpersonal archetypes. In this way, historic formulations of the Trinity are rejected in favor of formulas more acceptable to those who seek to incorporate a radical feminism into their theology.

The second point of The Declaration affirms the full deity and full humanity of Jesus Christ. It affirms Christ Jesus alone as the way to reconciliation with God. Among UCC trends countered by this point are the following: 1) a theological pluralism which, contrary to Scripture, declares that there are many different ways by which humans may attain salvation and reconciliation with God; 2) assorted denials of the deity of Jesus Christ or equally serious confusions about His genuine humanity; 3) assertions that human beings can by their own works achieve a righteousness that will satisfy God; and 4) erroneous views that human effort is sufficient to establish the Kingdom of God.[3]

The third point declares that "the Bible is the written Word of God, the infallible rule of faith and practice for the church of Jesus Christ." This point challenges a chief tenet of theological radicals in the UCC. It affirms the rule of Scripture and denies the claim of those who make human experience the final criterion of religious truth.

The fourth point affirms the central message of the Scriptures to be the Good News of reconciliation through the atoning sacrifice of Christ. It affirms salvation by grace alone and the call to works of piety, mercy, and justice. While Christians are called to a life of good works, they are not saved or reconciled by these works, which express the fact that they have been put in a right relationship with God through the sacrifice of Christ.

In the fifth point, The Declaration asserts its continuity with the great ecumenical creeds and Reformation confessions because they conform to the teaching of Holy Scripture. This point challenges the assertion of some that the UCC is a non-creedal church. These creeds and confessions were affirmed in the UCC Constitution and in the Basis of Union. They are still affirmed by many in the denomination. Those who would set these creeds and confessions aside are being unfaithful to the agreements made in the Union as well as to the teachings of those creeds and confessions, teachings that are founded on Scripture.

The sixth point declares a commitment to the "Great Commission." This was included to call the Church from its lethargy about the real nature of the Church's mission in the world.

Following the adoption of The Declaration, the Board decided to issue a call to the congregation to attend a convocation and organize a new movement. It also decided to produce a book that would serve as the basis for study of the major issues troubling the United Church of Christ. One justification for such a book was the Board's desire to counter the charge of denominational leaders that the movement had not documented its charges. A committee was formed to edit a draft of the book, subsequently published under the title *Affirming Our Faith*. The projected book would have a unique format, being divided into four columns. The first column would explain what the Bible teaches about the issue; the second would state the position of the historic Church and Protestant Reformers; the third column would provide specific documentation of the positions of the UCC leadership on the issue; and the final column would state the position of the Biblical Witness movement.

The Convocation, held in late June 1984 in Byfield, Massachusetts, was attended by more than four hundred people from every region of the United States. The meeting was filled with opportunities for worship, study, and fellowship. There was a resounding commitment to the need for an ongoing witness for renewal and reform in the United Church of Christ. The recommendations of the Planning Committee to establish a full-time executive director and a budget to carry forward and expand the work of the movement were approved. Also approved were a new constitution and a new name, the Biblical Witness Fellowship.

The Convocation made it clear that the new organization would work for renewal by beginning in the local churches and then letting the effort affect the other areas of the Church. This differed from the work of the UCPBW, which had been directed primarily at the level of the General Synod. Following the recommendation of the Planning Committee, the Convocation secured the services of Gerald Sanders as executive director. As chief administrative officer of the organization, the executive director would see to the day-to-day operations of the Fellowship and function as its public representative.[4]

The Board of Directors voted to publish *Affirming Our Faith* and to make it available to the churches of the denomination. The appearance of the book provoked an immediate response from the denominational leadership. The leadership objected to the book's mention of specific names. One member of the BWF Board observed that it was impossible to please the UCC leadership. When no names are given, the leadership accuses the BWF of issuing vague and unsupported charges; when names are listed, the BWF is accused of making personal attacks.

While the book did not make a big hit with the UCC bureaucracy, it was well received by the laity and by many clergy. It gave teeth to a fear felt for a long time that the denomination was out of step with what they understood their Church to be. After reading the book, one layman in Ohio said, "My Church is being stolen from me."

Positive response to the Biblical Witness Fellowship from the grass roots was immediate. The budget needs were underwritten, and membership grew to forty thousand financial supporters in the first six months.

Negative response was not long in coming from the denominational leadership. Someone began to circulate the false charge that the Biblical Witness Fellowship was out to split the Church. The Fellowship was accused of being schismatic, but the actual work of the Fellowship has proven this charge false. For one thing, the executive director, president, and other members of the Board have worked hard in an effort to encourage congregations to remain in the denomination. For another, membership in a UCC congregation is a necessary condition for membership in the Fellowship. If the Fellowship really were intent on schism, any success it might have would in effect reduce its own base of support. The charge of being schismatic is actually a "red herring" designed to avoid coming to terms with what is really driving congregations from the denomination: a bureaucracy whose radical stands have alienated many in the local churches.

The Biblical Witness Fellowship seeks to address several needs in the Church. One of these is the need of local congregations who desire to secure orthodox and evangelical pastoral leadership. Pastoral profiles supplied by the denomination's Office for Church Life and Leadership often make it difficult to identify the pastor's theological position. The BWF supplies to interested churches names of evangelical pastors who have contacted the BWF. Interested congregations may then secure the profiles of these candidates from their association minister. If they have problems getting the right profiles, they then contact the BWF office, which checks to see what is the problem. Currently the demand for evangelical-orthodox pastors exceeds the supply by three to one.

Another problem addressed by the BWF is the loss of young seminarians to more evangelical denominations. Many young people from UCC congregations preparing for the ministry feel that they have no place in their denomination because their evangelical beliefs do not square with what they perceive as the theological position of the denomination. The executive director, president, and members of the Board regularly visit seminary campuses to meet with evangelical UCC students. They encourage these students to remain in the UCC and work to help get them placed after graduation. The BWF also provides scholarship aid to seminary students who are supporters of the BWF.

The BWF leadership also works with Fellowship personnel in the various conferences and associations of the UCC. They seek to help them organize for action and ministry within their conference or association.

The BWF is often asked to direct local churches to centers of UCC missions that are clearly orthodox and evangelical in their vision. Such centers have received significant financial help as a result of BWF efforts. In one such case, the BWF was contacted by persons associated with the Southern Mindanao District Conference of the UCC in the Philippines. They wanted a seminary that would be affordable for students as well as being evangelical in theology. The UCC establishment in the Philippines was opposed to starting such a school. Opposition from some powerful persons in the UCC in the United States was also apparent. While the BWF would have preferred that the UCC respond to a request from a sister church, it was unwilling to sit by and see this need ignored. The BWF therefore has worked with the Southern Mindanao District to establish the seminary, now operating in Davao City. It is actively seeking to raise capital for the new school.

The Biblical Witness Fellowship has continued to monitor issues of importance to the United Church of Christ. One such concern is the issue of financial accountability. The denominational leadership has failed to provide satisfactory answers to inquiries about what programs the UCC was supporting or the amount of financial support it was giving. The BWF has been active in alerting local churches to this problem, as well as providing advice to local churches and individuals interested in pressuring the National Offices to provide more complete and accurate reporting. While the National Office finally appointed a committee to address the issue and has begun to unify its reporting of expenditures, there are still no plans to provide specific and comprehensive line item reporting of expenditures. The BWF has formed a Committee on Financial Accountability to address this problem. The committee, composed of leading business and professional people in the UCC, is presently developing material that will help more members of the UCC become aware of this problem. Unless the UCC bureaucracy takes responsible action in this matter, it will do even more to undermine the trust of local congregations.

The General Synod of the United Church of Christ has continued to drift towards the radical left. At its last meeting in June 1984, the Synod adopted the most radical stand yet on human sexuality. It voted to become an "Open and Affirming Church." This meant that the Synod was calling on every level of the UCC to incorporate persons with a homosexual orientation into the life and ministry of the Church. The Synod voted to bring to reality its radical agenda on inclusive language and other programs that cannot help but increase the alienation of many local congregations from the leadership. In the view of the BWF, the radical opinions of the National Staff of the UCC would not find support in the majority of UCC congregations.

The UCC is a covenant Church. This means that the glue

holding it together is mutual trust and support. For a covenant to work, it is necessary that both parties share a common commitment with regard to the essential points in their relationship. The more distant the parties become on these major points, the weaker the covenant relationship becomes.

The BWF has asserted that this weakening of the covenant is bad for the welfare of the Church. What the UCC needs is a reformation in which the Synod becomes more representative of the local churches. When delegates are elected by conferences and associations, the people electing them seldom know where these candidates stand on the issues. If conference and association ministers trusted their congregtions enough to let them vote for delegates based on where those candidates stand on the issues, an important step towards strengthening the covenant will have been taken. What the conference and association leadership wants instead is a process of unenlightened voting, one mark of repressive rule. Those favoring unenlightened voting may continue to appeal to the "autonomy of the Synod" or assert that "the Synod speaks to the churches and not for them." But unless there is a change, the Synod's autonomy will become so complete that there will be no question that it speaks only for itself. It will then exist on its own, a situation that many in the UCC doubt is theologically justifiable. Whether the Synod could continue to receive the financial support it would need is unclear.

While seeking to be a voice for the welfare of the Church beyond the local parish, the vast amount of BWF time and money is spent on helping local congregations in the renewal process. The BWF sponsors programs of education and spiritual enrichment through biannual Convocations on Church Renewal, assistance to local congregations struggling with renewal in their own life, and encouragement to local pastors and congregations.

In late June 1986, the Biblical Witness Fellowship held its second Convocation on Church Renewal in St. Charles, Missouri. Under the general theme of the unity of the Church, the Convocation included more than twenty seminars ranging from theological issues to the development of ministries of evangelism and pastoral care. Approximately four hundred persons attended. The meeting witnessed to the power and commitment of the grass roots for reform renewal in the UCC. It witnessed to a love for the UCC and manifested the willingness of BWF supporters to make the sacrifices of time and money necessary to reverse the sad decline of the denomination in recent years.

While the Biblical Witness Fellowship is the largest and perhaps most developed ministry for renewal and reform in the UCC, several other movements are active in the Church. The Fellowship of Charismatic Christians in the United Church of Christ is the oldest and second largest renewal movement in the UCC. It has developed a number of programs which seek to minister to the needs of congregations. It holds annual meetings for worship and study. Led by a Board of Directors that oversees its ministry, the Fellowship has no paid staff and has not sought to be directly involved in the struggle for political reform in the UCC. It publishes a quarterly newsletter and participates in a number of ecumenical meetings on charismatic renewal.

The Fellowship of Charismatic Christians has recently developed a program to help local churches in the renewal process. It is based on the concept of developing lay witness ministries within the life of the congregation and community. This program has enjoyed great success. "Acts Alive" is available to congregations irregardless of the congregation's involvement with the FCC. It is growing to the point that the greatest need at present is for additional leaders to work in congregations.

The Biblical, Liturgical, Theological Fellowship is another group in the UCC which might be considered a movement for renewal. It grows out of the desire of some in the German Reformed tradition to uphold the insights of Mercersburg theology. This was a liturgical-theological development in the German Reformed Church in the middle of the nineteenth century. The BLT has remained largely confined to Pennsylvania and has focused on meetings for scholarly discussion and debate around issues related to Mercersburg. It has not been involved widely in the life of the Church.

A group concerned with theological debate and dialogue in the UCC is centered at the Craigville Conference Center on Cape Cod. While this group has issued a number of statements, it is not directly involved in the life of local churches and it is still unclear what direction this group will take. Its meetings often include representatives of every theological viewpoint in the UCC.

The newest group to form is the Spiritual Life Network. This group developed under the leadership of Dr. Bernie Zerkel, an association minister who was concerned about spiritual development in the life of the Church. This group has held meetings and issued some public statements. It is unclear to what extent this group will relate to local congregations, although it does have the support of the national denominational leaders. While some evangelicals in the UCC are sympathetic to the concerns of the Spiritual Life Network, its programs have included lectures on Native American religion, Eastern religions, and other non-Christian approaches to spirituality, in addition of course to the expected lectures on classic Christian spirituality. SLN seems clearly headed in the direction of theological pluralism.

It is too early to say what is going to happen in the UCC. It is clear that the days of blind trust and congregational disengagement are over. The real future of the denomination seems to turn on whether the covenant can be reestablished.

It is clear that the UCC has come to a fork in the road. If the denominational officers and their supporters refuse to open the Church to the grass roots, they will only continue to erode their support among the congregations. Evangelical leaders believe that real renewal can come only through faithfulness to the truth revealed in the Holy Scriptures and confessed through the ages. Unless the denominational leaders end their efforts to change that message, evangelicals believe the denomination will continue to decline.

THE DUBUQUE DECLARATION

We declare our continuing commitment to the truths set forth in the Basis of Union and the Constitution of the United Church of Christ.

We perceive an erosion and denial of these truths in our church. Because of our concern for the people of our churches and the well-being of our denomination as a member of the body of Christ, we are called by God to make this confession:

1) We confess our faith in the triune God—Father, Son, and Holy Spirit.

2) We confess that Jesus Christ is truly God and truly man. Because of our sin and estrangement from God, at the Father's bidding the Son of God took on flesh. Conceived by the Holy Spirit and born of the Virgin Mary, He became like us in all things apart from sin. He died on the cross to atone for our sin and reconcile us to God and on the third day rose bodily from the dead. He is the sole head of the church, the Lord and Savior of us all, and will one day return in glory, power, and judgment to usher in the kingdom of God in its fullness.

3) We hold that the Bible is the written Word of God, the infallible rule of faith and practice for the church of Jesus Christ. The Scriptures have binding authority on all people. All other sources of knowing stand under the judgment of the Word of God.

4) We affirm that the central content of the Scriptures is the gospel of reconciliation and redemption through the atoning sacrifice of Christ and His glorious resurrection from the grave. The good news is that we are saved by the grace of God alone, the grace revealed and fulfilled in the life and death of Jesus Christ, which is received only by faith. Yet this faith does not remain alone but gives rise to works of piety, mercy, and justice. The Holy Spirit, who spoke through the prophets and apostles, calls us today, as in the past, to seek justice and peace for all races, tongues and nations.

5) We confess as our own the faith embodied in the great ecumenical and Reformation creeds and confessions, finding them in basic conformity with the teaching of the Holy Scriptures.

6) We confess that the mission of the church is to bear witness to God's law and gospel in our words and deeds. We are sent into the world as disciples of Christ to glorify God in every area of life and to bring all peoples into submission to the Lordship of Christ, baptizing them in the name of the Father and of the Son and of the Holy Spirit. We seek to obey this commission in the full assurance that our Lord and Savior is with us always, even to the end of the age.

—Adopted by the Board of Directors of
United Church People for Biblical Witness,
Dubuque, Iowa, November 17, 1983

A DIRECTORY OF RENEWAL GROUPS IN THE UNITED CHURCH OF CHRIST

The address for the Biblical Witness Fellowship is P.O. Box 50384, Knoxville, Tennessee 37950-0384. Its telephone number is 615/986-5962. Rev. Gerald Sanders is executive director. The BWF publishes *The Witness,* a bimonthly newsletter, and *Living Faith,* a quarterly journal. It has also published two books, *Issues in Sexual Ethics* and *Affirming Our Faith.*

The Fellowship of Charismatic Christians in the UCC may be reached in care of P.O. Box 12, Sassamansville, Pennsylvania 19472. Rev. Vernon Stoops, Jr. is director of services.

The address for the Biblical Liturgical Theological Study Group is 300 W. Third Avenue, Trappe, Pennsylvania 19426.

KEVIN PERROTTA
is associate director of the
Center for Pastoral Renewal
in Ann Arbor, Michigan, and
managing editor of the
Center's monthly publication,
Pastoral Renewal. A graduate
of the University of
Michigan, Perrotta has
written articles for such
journals as *America, Eternity,*
and *New Oxford Review.* He
is co-editor of several books
including *Christianity
Confronts Modernity,
Summons to Faith and
Renewal,* and *Christianity in
Conflict.*

EIGHT
The U.S. Catholic Church
Kevin Perrotta

A n account of renewal in the Roman Catholic Church at the end of the 1980s naturally takes its point of departure from the great call to renewal in the Catholic Church in this century—the Second Vatican Council. The years from 1962 to 1965, when the Council met, through the end of 1985, when a special synod of bishops gathered in Rome to take stock of successes and failures in the implementation of the Council, constitute a distinct period, a watershed, in the life of the contemporary Catholic Church. Following the 1985 synod, the Catholic Church, in the U.S. and elsewhere, entered a new phase. An understanding of this phase may begin with a brief review of the Council and what followed it.

The overriding purpose of Vatican Council II was to enable the Catholic Church to bear more effective witness to Christ in the modern world. Toward this evangelistic end, the bishops envisioned several necessary steps.

One was to move the Church beyond what had been in some ways a defensive stance toward the modern world. Without denying the many positive contributions of the Catholic Church in the first half of the century—among which the popes' development of Catholic social teaching and the expansion of missionary work in the Third World were two notable achievements—the Catholic Church carried into the pontificate of John XXIII (1958-63) a posture of defensiveness against modern social and political movements. Much of the background for this lay in the extreme forms of anticlericalism and conflicts with anti-Christian governments with which the Catholic Church had had to deal in Europe from the time of the French Revolution. In order to present the gospel persuasively in a new age, the bishops wished to express an appreciation for modern values which deserved at least qualified Christian endorsement, such as the human longing for human freedom, the sense of the interdependence of peoples in the "global village," and men's and women's desire to exercise political responsibility for their own lives. The early 1960s, which witnessed the flowering of the postwar European economic miracle and saw a Catholic occupying the White House, seemed an appropriate moment for Catholics to take as favorable a view as possible of modern culture.

As a second step toward their goal, the bishops saw the need to update the structures and forms of Church life. Canon law, the Church's code of rules and regulations, needed to be adapted to modern circumstances. Structures of shared responsibility were needed to enable laypeople to participate fully in the mission of the Church.

Thirdly, the Christian message needed to be articulated in a way suited to the patterns of thought and the questions of modern people. The Council produced two major statements of the Christian faith, one of which explored the implications of the gospel for the modern world and was addressed not only to believers but to all men and women.

In articulating the Christian faith for the twentieth century, the bishops did not have to respond to any particular major doctrinal challenge. In Church history, confrontation with doctrinal challenges has played a key role in clarifying Christian teaching. However, the necessity of responding to challenges often produces partial rather than comprehensive answers. At Vatican II the bishops enjoyed a unique opportunity to state their understanding of the gospel in a positive, nonpolemical way. Considering the profound controversies which, as will be described, broke out even as the Council drew to a close, it is fortunate that the bishops took the opportunity.

Finally, the bishops saw that the Catholic Church as a whole needed to renew itself through a deeper contact with the sources of spiritual life. The Council capped movements for Scriptural and liturgical renewal that developed between the World Wars. The Council directed that the Scriptures should be restored to a prominent place in the daily life of Church members. The liturgy and the administration of the sacraments should be stripped of accretions of recent centuries so that their fundamental lines appeared more clearly to view. Thus they would become more transparent to the presence of Christ, and Catholics would be able to enter more easily into the saving mystery of His death and resurrection. The bishops directed that both the Scriptures and the liturgy should be available to Catholics in their everyday languages. The many religious orders were directed to renew themselves in light of their original charisms and purposes.

Church renewal requires teaching, changes in structures, and then appropriation in life. In Vatican Council II the Catholic bishops presented teaching and mandated changes. By 1983, with the completion of the new code of canon law, the Council's structural and liturgical reforms were largely in place. However, the picture was mixed regarding appropriation of this renewal in life, what might be regarded as *real* renewal. In the United States after the Council, while many individual Catholics experienced renewal, and movements of spiritual renewal and evangelism arose, much ground that seemed firmly held was lost.

The Council's attempt to acknowledge whatever was good in the modern world, and to purify it through the gospel, coincided with American Catholics' massive entry into the mainstream of American life. The period of major Irish, Italian, and Slavic immigration that formed ethnic Catholic enclaves in the northern cities had ended in 1920, and by the 1960s third-generation American Catholics were sharing in the mass suburban culture equally with Protestants. The message of the Council, which seemed to call for openness to the world, and the opportunities to share equally in American life combined to reorient many Catholics' thinking about their relationship with American society. The motivation to maintain Catholic distinctiveness through separate schools and organizations faded. The tendency grew to see Catholics' mission in efforts to build the secular society (this was the period of Harvey Cox's widely read *Secular City*). Church and world no longer seemed so far apart.

Unfortunately, these developments also coincided with a new wave of de-Christianization in American life, more powerful than any since the 1920s. Catholics let down their guard just at the moment when family life was losing its honored place in American culture, the sexual revolution was entering a more radical phase, selfism was being proclaimed more blatant-ly, the secular feminist movement was being launched, and the tone of public life was becoming more hostile than ever before to Christian values. Entering the mainstream, many Catholics were carried along by these powerful anti-Christian currents. Consequently, the Council's call for personal and corporate renewal, renewal in relationship with Christ and His Word, was actually followed by widespread confusion and loss of commitment in the Catholic Church in the U.S.

The plan after the Council was that Catholics would move from a piety too heavily dependent on rules and customs to a deeper sanctity based on greater personal faith and conviction. But when the props of devotion and identity were removed— laws of fasting in Lent and abstinence from meat on Fridays, various popular devotions, and so on—many Catholics found themselves increasingly adrift. Indeed, for many American Catholics in the 1960s and 1970s rote piety and moral legalism were not replaced by deeper conversion to Christ, but rather their abandonment was followed by further abandonment of life commitments and of basic Christian doctrines and moral teaching. This process showed that religious practices and tokens of identity play a more important role in religious life than many people thought. Moreover, it revealed a preexisting weakness in many Catholics' spiritual life which was not adequately addressed after the Council—although various renewal movements, described below, did appear.

Most dramatic of the flights from religious constraints during the 1960s and 1970s were the sharp drop in regular attendance at the Sunday liturgy (from three-quarters attending to only one-half attending), an exodus of priests (some ten thousand resigned between 1966 and 1978) and men and women from religious orders, and a sudden decline in the numbers of young men and women seeking to become priests or religious sisters or brothers. The exodus of religious sisters and the drying up of the stream of applicants was so severe that the total number of sisters fell from about one hundred eighty thousand in 1965 to about one hundred ten thousand in 1985, creating a crisis in the Catholic school system, which had depended on the sisters' dedicated service. Thousands of schools closed and enrollment shrank by more than a third between 1965 and 1983.

By the middle of the 1980s the percentage of Catholics

attending church regularly had stabilized at a level much lower than before the Council. The exodus of priests and sisters had slowed, but the number of applicants remained below replacement level of those retiring. Some religious congregations of women were made up largely of older women, and some of these groups seemed bound for extinction. Thus, while the number of Americans who identify themselves as Catholics was larger than ever, their degree of commitment, as evidenced in faithfulness to corporate worship and willingness to leave all to serve the Kingdom of God, was much less than it was before the council.

Entering the mainstream of American life just as the current was flowing more rapidly away from Christianity, Catholics lost much of their Christian way of life. Survey research indicates that the sexual revolution of the 1960s and 1970s profoundly affected Catholics' sexual attitudes and behavior. Catholic young people, for example, rejected Christian teaching against sexual relations outside marriage. Catholic couples went through divorce in record numbers—indeed, at a rate *exceeding* for a time that of the general population, suggesting a "catching-up effect" by Catholics who previously felt inhibited from divorcing in the Catholic subculture but who now felt free to do so. A national organization of Catholics promoting abortion appeared, as did two national organizations of Catholic homosexuals which did not regard the Christian prohibition of homosexual practice as an absolute.

In an unforeseen way, Catholics' abandonment of basic Christian moral principles may have been accelerated by the positive changes that flowed from Vatican Council II. Once introduced into a stable theological and liturgical situation, the very dynamic of change fostered a mentality of uncertainty regarding what was not changeable and an expectation that one change would inevitably lead to another. If Latin, the language of the liturgy from time out of mind, could disappear overnight, what might disappear tomorrow? If Catholics could now eat meat on Friday, would they soon be able to divorce? The secular media promoted the notion that "progressive" forces were moving toward the loosening of such moral restraints. Priest-sociologist Andrew Greeley charted the appearance of a considerable sector of American Catholicism, which he called the communal Catholics, who continue to feel themselves a part of the Catholic Church but who feel free to accept or reject any aspect of the Church's communication of the Christian revelation and its moral demands.

Not easily measurable but clearly evident was Catholics' embrace of consumerist and careerist values. The symptoms were observable among Catholics as among other Americans— a valedictorian boasting at a Catholic high school commencement of the expensive postgraduation trip planned by her classmates, a largely Catholic union local voting against a company offer to reduce overtime in order to rehire laid-off fellow workers, mothers leaving infants in day-care centers to pursue professional careers.

Of course, this is not to say that all Catholics abandoned Christian teaching. Many remained faithful; many even experienced renewal. But the predominant direction of change was toward secularization. By the mid-1980s the Catholic Church in America was in greater need of evangelical renewal—renewal through repentance and faith in Christ—than twenty-five years before. If many Catholics continued to stand in need of the conversion intended by Vatican II from a superficial and routine form of Christianity, many also needed to hear the gospel call to turn from a worldly life and rediscover Christ's power to bring personal, family, and social transformation.

An important factor in the secularization of American Catholics was development among the middle leadership of the church—priests and lay theologians, religious sisters and brothers. At the Council the bishops did not alter anything fundamental in Christian teaching. Their intention was rather to restate the basics in a way that was both Scriptural and up to date. But after the Council, Catholic theologians in the U.S. lost their unanimity. Virtually every aspect of historic Christian teaching was widely questioned. In some quarters, certainty about historic Christian teaching was replaced by certainty about Christians' obligation to join in particular political and social causes. Catholic priests and religious sisters became some of the most dogmatic Catholic proponents of the Equal Rights Amendment, the Sandinista revolution, and the antinuclear weapons movement.

American Catholic theologians' widespread dissent from received Christian teaching, especially in the moral sphere, was especially debilitating because it came at a time when faithfulness to Christian values and moral principles was becoming more difficult. When certainty and clarity in preaching and teaching would have been most helpful, Church elites' uncertainty (and perhaps their fear of alienating people) led them to mute their preaching and to accept ambiguities in religious education materials. Catholics found themselves caught up in the midst of an intense secular cultural revolution affecting every aspect of sexual behavior—abortion, fornication, adultery, divorce, masturbation, artificial contraception, homosexual practice. But they heard very little from most Catholic pulpits on the subject. Rather than hearing an appeal to traditional Christian values concerning family life, for instance, Catholics might open a pastoral letter from their bishop on the role of women in Church and society to find an echo of the secular feminist movement, with only a passing reference to the family. Catholic magazines and books carried the message that while official Catholic teaching on various issues had not changed, it was no longer binding, since Vatican Council II supposedly had promulgated a new view of conscience (an instance of appealing to the "spirit" of the Council rather than to what it actually said). Catholics were told that reliable theologians now took a range of other views, and Catholics needed to make a "responsible" choice between the official teaching and the competing approaches.

While the theological ferment seemed to some observers as a kind of Protestant rejection of the teaching office of the pope and the role of tradition in favor of an appeal to conscience, the similarities between the historic Reformers and the modern Catholic dissenters were only superficial. The Protestant Reformers rejected a papacy that they perceived as failing to preach the gospel of salvation by faith; they rejected Church traditions as aberrations from the supremely authoritative teaching of Scripture. But recent Catholic theologians who have questioned the teaching authority of the pope and traditional Catholic formulations of Christian faith have generally advocated reinterpretations of Christianity which are essentially similar to those of secularizing Protestant theologians. Thus many contemporary Catholic and Protestant theologians find the supernatural aspects of Christian teaching implausible for modern men and women, are uncomfortable with the exclusive claims of historic Christianity, see the Scriptures as basically

human and culture-bound religious documents, downplay the
effects of the fall of man and the need for personal faith in
Christ, and recast the Christian message in terms of feminism
or leftist revolution. Perhaps unexpectedly from the point of
view of Protestant observers, an aspect of Catholicism of which
Protestants have historically been particularly critical—the
teaching office of the pope—became one of the strongest supports for maintaining an understanding of the Christian faith
that would be recognizable to the Reformers.

The American Catholic bishops bore some responsibility
for the confused theological situation. Their acquiescence in
the teaching and publishing of views at odds with Catholic
doctrine was explained in part by their sense that authoritarian
methods of leadership had been retired after the Council: dialogue and discussion were to be allowed, and experimentation
was the order of the day, in theology as in liturgical practice. (In
some cases bishops seemed positively to favor unorthodox
views. Archbishop Raymond Hunthausen of Seattle put his
imprimatur on a work of moral theology that concluded that
homosexual practice and premarital sex were sometimes moral.
Archbishop John Quinn of San Francisco allowed a council of
clergy and laypeople in his archdiocese to express very sharp
criticisms of Christian teaching against homosexual practice.
Archbishop Peter Gerety of Newark put his seal of approval on
a catechism which the Vatican later found to have serious
doctrinal flaws.)

Another factor contributing to bishops' hesitation to act
decisively against those who undermined confidence in historic
Christian doctrines and moral positions was the bishops' strong
inclination to act in concert rather than individually on issues of
common concern. It became clear that taking action against
theologians who rejected aspects of Catholic teaching would
put an individual bishop in a position of isolation among his
brethren. Bishops may have been reluctant to anger priests at a
time when priests were in increasingly short supply. And some
bishops thought that Rome needed to take the initiative in
dealing with widespread dissent, since individual bishops were
not well-equipped to deal with professional theologians whose
departures from received Christian teaching often seemed quite
sophisticated.

The initiative for changing the situation thus lay with

Rome. During the late 1960s and 1970s the Vatican was aware of the problems in Catholic life throughout the West and acutely conscious of the need to restore Catholic theology to a clear, united presentation of the gospel. In 1977 Paul VI impressed on ninety visiting American bishops their responsibility to be faithful to the word of God:

> The word of God is the message that we proclaim; it is the criterion of our preaching; it is light and direction for the lives of our people. We have no hope outside God's word. Apart from it there are no valid solutions to the problems of our day. The faithful preaching of God's word—in all its purity, with all its exigencies, in all its power—constitutes the highest priority of our ministry, because all else depends on this. Aware of its relevance in our day, we do not hesitate to repeat the solemn charge Paul made to Timothy . . . "Proclaim the message and, welcome or unwelcome, insist on it" (2 Tim. 4:2). . . . And with a realistic awareness of certain challenges today to Catholic teaching, not least of which is in the field of sexual morality, we add: "Far from being content with sound teaching, people will be avid for the latest novelty and collect themselves a whole series of teachers according to their own tastes; and then, instead of listening to the truth, they will turn to myths. Be careful always to choose the right course; be brave under trials; make the preaching of the good news your life's work, in thoroughgoing service" (verses 3-5). . . . The most profound pastoral understanding, the deepest human compassion, exist only in fidelity to God's word. There is no division, no dichotomy, no opposition between God's commands and our pastoral service. . . . Speak about [the content of the faith] often to your people; discuss it with your priests and deacons and religious. We ask you to fulfill with loving personal attention your great pastoral responsibility to your seminarians: know the content of their courses, encourage them to love the word of God and never be ashamed of the seeming folly of the cross.[1]

Despite Paul VI's insight into the situation, strong action to deal with the pastoral and theological weaknesses of the Catholic Church in America and throughout the West came only with the accession of John Paul II. His strenuous global travels were motivated by a desire to preach the gospel directly and personally throughout the world. Without relinquishing the Vatican Council's vision of greater collegial cooperation between pope and bishops—illustrated in the regular bishops' synods in Rome—John Paul began exercising strong leadership in several ways. Particularly notable were his encyclical letters, in which he taught about Christ the redeemer of mankind, the role of the Holy Spirit, and other key subjects. His strategy moved him from an initial period in which he placed heavy emphasis on the need for holiness among clergy to a period of emphasis on holiness among laypeople, especially regarding family life, which he made the topic of an encyclical, and in regard to sexuality, which he preached on for more than a year at his weekly public audiences.

Of particular importance for the Catholic Church in the U.S. was the trend in John Paul's appointment of bishops. In the 1980s key dioceses began to go to men who were quite clear about the need for Catholic institutions to be faithful to fundamental Christian doctrine and who were themselves strong leaders. Prime examples were the appointment of Bernard Law to the Boston archdiocese, John O'Connor to the New York archdiocese, and Theodore McCarrick to the Newark archdiocese. These men demonstrated a willingness to face public opposition—witness Cardinal O'Connor's 1984 anti-abortion stance against New York Governor Mario Cuomo and Congresswoman Geraldine Ferraro (both Catholics), and his confrontation with the city of New York over a gay liberation ordinance. These bishops embraced the Catholic Church's social teaching, which seems at some points conservative but at other points not conservative at all.

Thus the secular press, which usually views Church leaders in terms of political ideology, had difficulty categorizing these men, who seemed to be an odd blend of liberal and conservative. For instance, Archbishop Roger Mahony of Los Angeles, a doctrinal conservative and an outspoken foe of abortion, also quickly became an aggressive advocate of better treatment for the many Hispanics in his diocese. By the middle of the 1980s it seemed that the leadership of such bishops might be especially crucial within the body of American bishops, where they would be unlikely to passively accept policies advocated by staff members or theologians allowing doctrinal deviations or politicization of the Church's message and mission.

In another expression of leadership, John Paul summoned an extraordinary synod of bishops in November-December 1985 to assess the life of the Catholic Church since Vatican Council II's close twenty years before. The synod faced honestly the positive and negative trends in the Church since the Council and the changes in the world situation.

The bishops acknowledged that to some degree the Church had failed to "distinguish between a legitimate openness to the world and the acceptance of a secularized world's mentality and order of values." This undiscerning openness had come at a time when "in the wealthy nations, we see the constant growth of an ideology characterized by pride in technical advances and a certain immanentism that leads to the idolatry of material goods (so-called 'consumerism'). . . . In addition, we cannot deny the existence in society of forces capable of great influence that act with a certain hostile intention toward the church. All of these things manifest the work of the 'prince of this world' and of the 'mystery of iniquity,' even in our day."

The bishops followed this sober observation with the remark that the secularized culture of the West showed signs of exhaustion and "a thirst for the transcendent and divine." The question the bishops posed, however, was how clearly the Church was showing the face of Christ to a spiritually hungry world. "Have we not perhaps," the bishops asked, spoken "too much of the renewal of the church's external structures and too little of God and of Christ? . . . The church makes herself more credible if she speaks less of herself and ever more preaches Christ crucified and witnesses with her own life."

The bishops renewed the Vatican Council's emphasis that the preaching of the gospel is the Church's central task. And they spoke of the need for personal holiness in the lives of all the members in order to make this possible. Structural renewal, the bishops said, was of first importance no longer—if it had ever been. Rather, "Today, we have tremendous need of saints." In the synod's typically realistic tone, the bishops noted that evangelization must begin at home. "Evangelization of nonbelievers presupposes the self-evangelization of the baptized and also, in a certain sense, of deacons, priests, and bishops."

The synod recognized that the evangelization of the young was particularly jeopardized. "Everywhere on earth today, the transmission to the young of the faith and the moral values deriving from the gospel is in danger."

In a brief but clear and significant statement on Catholic theology since the Council, the bishops expressed their "regret that the theological discussions of our day have sometimes occasioned confusion among the faithful."

The synod's emphasis on going beyond the structural changes of the previous twenty-five years to attain the spiritual renewal those changes were designed to facilitate was expressed quite forcefully a few months before the synod by Cardinal Joseph Ratzinger in a book-length interview with journalist Vittoria Messori (published in the U.S. as *The Ratzinger Report* by Ignatius Press). "The true time of Vatican II has not yet come," he told an interviewer. "Its authentic reception has not yet begun. . . . Every council, in order to really bear fruit, must be followed by a wave of holiness." Ratzinger's views are particularly noteworthy because of his position as prefect of the Congregation for the Doctrine of the Faith, a job which makes him arguably the number two man after the pope in the leadership of the Catholic Church.

Ratzinger spoke of the need for the Catholic Church to embrace a boldly countercultural stance. "After the phase of indiscriminate 'openness' it is time that the Christian reacquire the consciousness of belonging to a minority and of often being in opposition to what is obvious, plausible, and natural for that mentality which the New Testament calls—and certainly not in a positive sense—the 'spirit of the world.' It is time to find again the courage of nonconformism, the capacity to oppose many of the trends of the surrounding culture."

Both the synod and Ratzinger spoke positively of movements of spiritual renewal arising in the Catholic Church in recent years. "The apostolic movements and new movements of spirituality are the bearers of great hope," the bishops at the synod said. "Because the church is communion, the new 'basic communities,' if they truly live in unity with the church, are a true expression of communion and the means for the construction of a more profound communion." Ratzinger was more specific. "What is hopeful at the level of the universal church—

and what is happening right in the heart of the crisis of the church in the Western world—is the rise of new movements which nobody planned and which nobody has called into being, but which have sprung spontaneously from the inner vitality of the faith itself. What is manifested in them—albeit subdued—is something like a Pentecostal season in the church. I am thinking, say, of the charismatic movement, of the Cursillos, of the movement of the Focolare, of the neo-catechumenal communities, of Communion and Liberation, etc. . . . I find it marvelous that the Spirit is once more stronger than our programs and brings himself into play in an altogether different way than we had imagined." Nevertheless, Ratzinger added, "for the present, still prevalent trends are in fact moving in an altogether different direction. If one looks at the 'general meterological situation' of the Spirit, we must speak of a crisis of faith and of the church. We can overcome it only if we face up to it forthrightly."

Thus by the end of 1985 the Catholic Church in the U.S. and around the world entered a new stage. The thrust toward renewal was articulated at the highest levels of Catholic leadership. The postsynod agenda called for preaching the gospel. This would involve an emphasis on personal conversion to Christ, holiness of life, and movements of the Spirit bringing renewal and community. It would require frank acknowledgment of the conflict between Christianity and secular culture in the West and confrontation with trends in Catholic teaching and institutions that blur or distort the preaching of the gospel and its implications for Christian discipleship. The clarity of this agenda—and the theological sophistication, cultural awareness, and strength of leadership of men at the highest levels of Catholic Church leadership who defined it—was itself a work of the Spirit, still seeking to bring forth the renewal launched a quarter of a century before at the Vatican Council.

While the correction of aberrations in teaching would not itself accomplish renewal in Christian life any more than structural changes alone could, the challenge of correction would have to be faced forthrightly if renewal of life in faithfulness to the gospel was ever to be possible. In 1986, two corrective efforts were the Vatican's discipline of Father Charles Curran, a moral theologian at Catholic University of America, and the

Vatican's progress toward a policy requiring adherence to orthodox teaching and uprightness of life by those teaching theology in Catholic institutions of higher learning.

After Father Curran refused to recant his publicly stated views on the permissibility of homosexual practice, premarital sex, divorce, and other sexual behavior contrary to Catholic teaching, the Vatican withdrew his privilege to teach as a Catholic theologian. His case was especially significant because twenty years before, Father Curran had led the charge against Pope Paul VI's reassertion of Catholic teaching against artificial contraception—Curran's being the first act of open dissent that opened the way to many others by American Catholic theologians in the years that followed. Father Curran thus represented the American Catholic theological establishment's rejection of traditional Catholic moral teaching on sex. In disciplining him, the Vatican was not only signaling the whole Catholic Church that Catholic teaching on sex had not changed and was not going to change, but was also demonstrating to the Catholic academic community that those who officially represent the Catholic Church do not have the right to teach views in conflict with its teaching. Significantly, hundreds of American theologians protested the move against Father Curran.

The prospective Vatican policy regarding those who teach Catholic theology in Catholic institutions represented a systematic way of dealing with the same problem. The rule would merely express the long-standing Catholic approach that those who teach Catholic theology must not only be academically qualified but must also communicate it faithfully and live it. In 1986, one hundred ten of the two hundred thirty-five presidents of Catholic colleges and universities in the U.S. protested the prospective rule. They claimed that criteria such as doctrinal orthodoxy and uprightness of life were too "vague" to be implemented—an objection that said something about their view of the definiteness of the Christian faith. They also argued that academic freedom barred such an intrusion into the inquiries of scholars—an objection which said something about their view of the truth-value of the Christian revelation and of man's ability, with God's grace, to attain reliable knowledge about God.

Catholic colleges and universities are generally independent

of direct control by the bishops. How the bishops could en-
force such a rule, given the absolute opposition of administra-
tors and faculties, loomed as a major question. Rather than
bringing the theology faculties back to faithfulness to historic
Christian doctrine and morality, the new rule, it seemed, might
lead instead to a clarification of the fact that many Catholic
institutions of higher learning do not accept any responsibility
for offering Catholic teaching in their doctrinal and moral
courses. Thus, after considerable furor, the rule might result in
a *de jure* acknowledgement of the current *de facto* secularization of Catholic colleges and universities. Refusing to submit to
the rule, some institutions would have to stop using "Catholic"
as part of their title.

This would represent a tremendous institutional loss to the
Catholic Church. But it would be helpful for Catholics and
others who wished to know exactly what the Catholic Church
believes and teaches on crucial subjects such as the nature of
God, salvation in Christ, Christian mission, morality, the certainty of the Christian revelation, and other important questions. In the face of institutional intransigence, the bishops'
alternative would be to go on indefinitely allowing everyone to
teach what is right in their own eyes and call it Catholic teaching.

Such corrective exercises of authority would have a mainly
negative character, marking off what the Catholic Church does
not believe. The Catholic Church also faces theological challenges to positive action. In a way that was not the case when
the bishops assembled for Vatican Council II, the Catholic
Church, like the major Protestant churches, does now clearly
face profound doctrinal challenges to the historic understanding of the Christian faith revealed in the Scriptures and maintained from the Council of Chalcedon until the nineteenth
century. Ideological trends in theology—feminism, the blending
of Christianity with either Marxism or classical liberalism, secular trends in Scripture study, remissive trends in moral teaching all represent serious and historically novel departures from
Christian orthodoxy. They require creative but faithful Christian thinking. In all these areas, the theological challenge is
simple and evangelical: to understand, communicate, and apply
God's revelation in Christ as testified to by the Scriptures and

handed on in the tradition of the Church. The challenge is to grasp the word of God that gives life and has the power and authority to shape human life, and to distinguish it from secularizing counterfeits and distortions.

The challenge requires effort at every level of the Catholic Church. While the degree of confusion and uncertainty in regard to all these issues is great throughout the middle levels of academic and pastoral leadership in the Catholic Church in the U.S., there is intellectual vitality at every level also. The Pope and his closest collaborators—for example, Cardinal Joseph Ratzinger—have shown acute sensitivity to the location of the crucial battles in the confrontation of Christianity and contemporary Western secular culture. John Paul's extensive reflections on human sexuality in light of the Scriptures and the analyses of liberation in Christ and liberation theology which have come from Cardinal Ratzinger's office are two examples of first-class Christian thinking on crucial areas of concern for all Christians who seek to be faithful to the teaching of the Scriptures.

In a single chapter it is possible to touch only lightly on the intellectual endeavors by American Catholics in the areas of challenge. The 1980s have seen a resurgence of intellectual activity among Catholics who embrace historic Christian teaching. During the 1980s at least three Catholic intellectual periodicals appeared: *New Oxford Review,* edited by Dale Vree, in Berkeley, California; *Fidelity,* edited by E. Michael Jones, in South Bend, Indiana; and *Crisis* (originally *Catholicism in Crisis*), edited by Philip Lawler, also in South Bend. The Fellowship of Catholic Scholars, founded in 1978 by historian James Hitchcock, Msgr. George A. Kelly, and others, showed signs of attracting bright young Catholic thinkers from various scholarly disciplines. The Franciscan University of Steubenville, in Ohio, began hosting small annual theological symposia which offered an embryonic alternative to the gatherings of the established Catholic Theological Society of America, which identified itself with a policy of dissent from the Catholic Church's presentation of Christian teaching.

On the broader, popular level, organizations and movements of renewal appeared which aimed at communicating the gospel and bringing people to a deeper conversion to Christ. As Joseph Ratzinger noted, the Spirit has been at work at the grass roots. Again, it is possible to merely touch briefly on a few examples.

The formal program that probably reached the largest number of Catholics during the 1970s and 1980s, at least to some degree, was Renew. A parish revitalization method, Renew involved small groups meeting over a period of two or three years, using prescribed discussion topics. The program called participants to deeper, more conscious personal faith in Christ and openness to the power of the Holy Spirit. It was developed in the Newark archdiocese and was adopted by many dioceses throughout the country. Catholic parishes tend to be quite large and generally suffer from a lack of involvement by most members. Any program which gives members an opportunity to get together and develop personal relationships is likely to be experienced as beneficial, and this dynamic may be one of the main reasons for enthusiasm over Renew.

While the program succeeded in helping some people come into a deeper relationship with the Lord, the results varied widely depending on the faith and maturity of the small-group leaders. Like any program, Renew could only be as effective as the people who run it. The program may be significant as an indication of Catholics' sense of need for evangelism and renewal, and also of their tendency to reply on programs that in practice often fail to get to the heart of the matter—effectively preaching the gospel in a way that brings people to a life-changing conversion to Christ.

By far the largest movement of renewal in the Catholic Church in America after Vatican Council II was charismatic renewal. The element of surprise and divine initiative was a major characteristic of the movement. Beginning among students and faculty at Duquesne and Notre Dame Universities in 1967, the movement spread very rapidly throughout the U.S., and from the U.S. to the Catholic Church throughout the world. During the 1970s the movement's ever growing conferences attracted considerable attention, especially those held annually at Notre Dame and Atlantic City, where attendance reached the thirty thousand to forty thousand range toward the end of the decade. During the 1980s the trend was toward smaller city-wide and state-wide gatherings, making more difficult an assessment of the numbers of Catholics involved, though one estimate put the figure at several hundred thousand. Opinion varies regarding whether, by the mid-1980s, the movement had peaked in numbers or was continuing to grow, although less dramatically.

The charismatic renewal meant a richer experience of God's presence and power for many already committed Catholics. For even larger numbers it was an opportunity to hear the gospel presented in a simple, direct manner, involving personal testimony to the action of God in the evangelist's life and an effective call to respond by turning to Christ and asking Him in faith for the power and gifts of the Spirit. The gospel, coming thus from other Catholics who had experienced a significant conversion themselves, had a great effect on many thousands of Catholics whose faith was weak or merely nominal.

The characteristic forms of the Catholic charismatic movement became home and parish prayer groups, served by diocesan renewal centers and a national service committee, renamed Chariscenter in 1986, with offices in South Bend, Indiana. The national office did not regulate or administer the charismatic renewal but recognised it to be a popular movement rather than an organization. Among other things Chariscenter has sponsored conferences and a directory of prayer groups and supporting organizations. The movement's major national publication, *New Covenant* magazine, moved its offices to Steubenville, Ohio, in 1986.

The Catholic charismatic renewal met with a remarkable degree of acceptance by the American bishops (and Catholic officials throughout the world , including at the Vatican). The bishops established a working committee to relate to the movement and repeatedly expressed their general approval of it. In their individual dioceses, the pattern developed of bishops designating a priest to act as liaison with the movement. While few bishops became involved themselves in the movement, they expressed pleasure at the movement's loyalty to the Catholic Church and appreciation of its evangelistic potential.

While evangelism, largely of Catholics themselves, was always a main thrust of the Catholic charismatic renewal, a deliberate focus on evangelism by those leading the movement in the mid-1980s represented a narrowing of the vision held by some who were leaders at its beginning. Many participants originally saw the movement as a divine initiative toward not only evangelism but also Church renewal, by reintroducing a wide range of gifts of the Spirit into Church life and by providing the spiritual power for bringing Christians together in strong commitment to each other. Thus the movement would restore to the Catholic Church some of the miraculous and communitarian character of the early Church. The harnessing of the Catholic charismatic renewal for evangelism gave the movement an outward thrust that, while consonant with its inner dynamic, meant a weakening of its inward thrust toward difficult but needed changes within the Church itself.

The conviction that the charismatic renewal was meant both to evangelize and build community in the Catholic Church led some of the early leaders to found "covenant communities." These groups affiliated with each other in various configurations. By the middle of the 1980s the more important ones were The Sword of the Spirit, with branches in Ann Arbor, Newark, Baltimore, and elsewhere; the People of Praise, with branches in South Bend, Minneapolis, and elsewhere; the Mother of God, in Washington, D.C.; and the People of God's Delight, in Dallas. The first two groups originated in the Catholic charismatic renewal but became explicitly interdenominational.

While numerically small, these communities have been significant for renewal in the Catholic Church—and other churches. They have modeled responses to the social situation that has led to the present crisis in Christian life in America. With a committed membership, a close-knit pattern of life, largely lay leadership, emphasis on practical Christian living day by day in the family, on the job, and so on, they have constituted strong social environments supporting members to live as Christians in a heavily secularized culture. Therefore the communities have seen themselves as pioneering approaches to maintaining a distinctive Christian life in contemporary society that may be of value to many other Christians. (The publication with which I am personally involved, *Pastoral Renewal,* an ecumenical monthly published by The Sword of the Spirit, has sought to communicate pastoral lessons learned in community life for a wider Church audience.)

Evangelism became a topic of interest in the American Catholic Church in the 1980s, although the results were hard to measure. The National Catholic Evangelization Association, headed by Father Alvin Illig, in Washington, D.C., began to publish evangelistic materials, drawing somewhat on insights of evangelical Protestants. Conferences sponsored by the organization attracted a wide variety of individuals and organizations for instructive and consciousness-raising "celebrations of evangelism." A magazine called *Catholic Evangelist* began publication in Miami in 1983 with the blessing of the local archbishop but went out of business after two years. Using a considerable array of the most up-to-date equipment, a convent of religious sisters in Birmingham, Alabama, led by Mother Angelica, launched the Eternal Word Television Network by satellite, reaching thousands of Catholics and others with evangelistic programming.

An older evangelistic organization on the scene was the Cursillo, founded in Spain after World War II and introduced in the U.S. in the early 1960s. The title is Spanish for "little course," from the three-day evangelistic retreat—a "little course" in Christianity—that is a keystone of the movement's method. The movement was stronger in the 1960s than in the 1980s. It is perhaps symptomatic of Catholic renewal efforts in the United States that the Cursillo movement here, as distinct from the movement in Spain and Latin America, tended to focus on the most dramatic and easiest to operate part of the Cursillo approach—the three-day weekend—and to lose sight of the patient individual and group development to which the "little course" was supposed to lead.

A new movement, FIRE, appeared in 1983. The title is an acronym for faith, intercession, repentance, and evangelism. Four Catholic charismatic renewal leaders joined to make up the "team"—Fathers Michael Scanlan and John Bertolucci, Ann Shields, and Ralph Martin. Through public rallies, follow-up meetings, and local chapters, they had directly affected some one hundred thousand Catholics by 1986, many of whom made a commitment to disciplines of prayer, Scripture study, and personal evangelism.

Several organizations appeared that were directed toward Spanish-speaking Catholics. One, Kerygma, was operating from a small office in Miami in 1986.

To summarize this brief reconnaissance of renewal in the Catholic Church in the U.S., the Vatican Council decreed changes that were designed to foster lay involvement, spiritual renewal, and evangelism—and which to some extent succeeded in doing so. However, through a confluence of factors the two decades after the Council were marked by a serious secularization of thought and life in the Catholic Church in the U.S., as well as elsewhere in the West. By the mid-1980s this situation was clearly recognized by the international leadership of the Catholic Church and an increasing number of U.S. bishops. Following the 1985 synod, the Catholic Church in the U.S. was entering a period of dealing with the problems that had arisen and of moving anew toward the goals of the Council. However, the situation seemed far less favorable than the one the Council was faced with. Great spiritual and theological resources, and signs of intellectual life and evangelism—even some powerful and promising development—seemed marginal in respect to the overall institutional and pastoral situation of the Catholic Church in the U.S.

God was clearly at work to bring renewal at the highest levels of Catholic leadership, at the grass roots, and at every level in between. But one must wonder whether a historical opportunity had not been lost, and whether God's work of renewal would not now involve more pain and loss than might otherwise have been the case. The ripening apostasy of the West from Christian faith and values after 1960 found the Catholic Church rather pliable and permeable to secular influences. Catholic scholars adopted secular values and sought the approval of secular authorities. Catholic clergy embraced secular ideological causes. Catholic families were shaped by the secular culture.

God often manifests His judgment by allowing the consequences of human foolishness to have their effect. The consequences in this case were a growing U.S. Catholic population with a shrinking number of priests and religious sisters, and a pattern of family breakdown that was as catastrophic as that of American society as a whole. A further consequence was a heightening of those influences that "act with a certain hostile intention toward the church" that the bishops noted at their 1985 synod. Perhaps in God's providence a Church that had not had the "courage of nonconformism" to "oppose many of the trends of the surrounding culture" was finding itself chastened by the culture it had not had the boldness to withstand.

Nevertheless, we may be sure that Christ, who lives in the Church and is its Head, is faithful to His own Body. If in the

1980s He was judging the Catholic Church, He is merciful in His severity, and Catholics could trust that He would bring forth the renewed life He had in mind.

A DIRECTORY OF RENEWAL GROUPS AND PUBLICATIONS IN THE CATHOLIC CHURCH

Catholics United for the Faith
45 Union Ave.
New Rochelle, New York 10801

The Center for Pastoral Renewal
John Blattner, Executive Director
P.O. Box 8617
Ann Arbor, Michigan 48107

Chariscenter
P.O. Box 1065
Notre Dame, Indiana 46556

Eternal Word Television Network
5817 Old Leeds Road
Birmingham, Alabama 35210

The Fellowship of Catholic Scholars
Msgr. George A. Kelly, Executive Secretary
St. John's University
Jamaica, New York 11439

FIRE
The Franciscan University of Steubenville
Franciscan Way
Steubenville, Ohio 43952

The Franciscan University of Steubenville
The Rev. Michael Scanlan, T.O.R., President
Franciscan Way
Steubenville, Ohio 43952

Kerygma
Pepe Alonso, Director
P.O. Box 55-7206
Miami, Florida 33255

The National Catholic Evangelization Association
The Rev. Alvin A. Illig, C.S.P., Director
The Paulist Fathers
3031 Fourth St., N.E.
Washington, D.C. 20017

National Committee of Catholic Laymen
150 E. 35th St.
New York, New York 10016

Communio
Gonzaga University
Spokane, Washington 99258

Crisis
P.O. Box 495
Notre Dame, Indiana 46556

Fidelity
206 Marquette Ave.
South Bend, Indiana 46617

New Covenant
P.O. Box 400
Steubenville, Ohio 43952

New Oxford Review
1069 Kains Ave.
Berkeley, California 94706

Pastoral Renewal
P.O. Box 8617
Ann Arbor, Michigan 48107

Evangelical Renewal—
The Next Step

The contributors to this book have discussed the present status of evangelical renewal in their denominations. The obvious question, as this book closes, concerns the next steps that people interested in renewal should take. This chapter will offer some suggestions to clergy and laypeople in three different groups: members of mainline churches who do not see themselves as evangelicals; members of mainline churches who are evangelicals; and evangelicals in other denominations.

A WORD TO NONEVANGELICALS IN MAINLINE CHURCHES

A great many people in mainline churches have no idea what evangelicalism is; many others have a distorted picture. Many laypeople, especially, are ungrounded in Scripture and Christian doctrine and are uninformed about the major theological changes that have taken place in their Church.

Many mainline Christians are good people who simply take the word of their Church or denominational leaders; they know no alternative to their Sunday school material; they know only the kind of preaching they hear in their own pulpit; they accept everything they read in their denominational literature.

Occasionally such people may catch an evangelical program on television and wonder at the differences between the messages of a Billy Graham and what they usually hear in their own Church. Slowly they may begin to wonder why the messages of evangelicals stir or move them.

Readers who may fall into this category should ask themselves some questions:

Do I believe in a personal, all-powerful, loving God who created the universe?

Do I believe that the Bible is God's inspired Word and that it is the standard by which Christian belief and practice should be judged?

Do I believe that Jesus Christ is the eternal Son of God who came into this world to die for my sins?

Do I believe that Jesus Christ rose bodily from the dead?

Do I believe that my only hope for forgiveness and eternal life is Jesus Christ and what He did for me in His death and resurrection?

Depending of course on the particular denomination, mainline Christians who believe all this are probably closer to evangelicalism than many leaders of their own denomination. It seems clear that many mainline Christians are evangelicals without knowing it.

Of course, many mainline Christians understand clearly what evangelicalism is and have decided to reject it and, possibly, to resist efforts to increase an evangelical presence within their denomination. It is not always clear, however, if those who reject evangelicalism do so for reasons that make sense, even from their perspective. For example, many nonevangelicals have picked up the idea that "old-fashioned Christianity" is no longer a plausible intellectual option in the modern world. Unfortunately, this rejection of evangelical Christianity results either from a serious misunderstanding of what evangelicalism is or an equally serious misunderstanding of what "modern scholarship" requires.

Evangelical Christianity does not conflict with any essential teaching of modern science, philosophy, or any other discipline for that matter. A scholarly approach to the Bible does not oblige sincere people to reject the Bible as a special revelation from God.[1]

Some insist on identifying evangelical Christianity with what they regard as substandard views on social justice or something of the sort. One's stance with respect to evangelicalism leaves open a wide variety of options with regard to social issues.[2] Becoming an evangelical does not necessarily oblige one to change his views on important social issues. It is important to keep distinct the nature of one's beliefs about God,

Jesus Christ, the Bible and conversion and the extremely complex questions of how one lives the Christian life in a fallen world. This book does not address the second set of questions.[3]

Evangelicals are not at war with modern science, culture, or technology. They are people who recognize that nothing that has transpired in the twentieth century compromises the early Christian convictions that men and women are sinners who need the forgiveness of God; that this salvation comes only through faith in the living Savior whose death and resurrection provided the ground of their redemption; and that the power for Christian living comes from God.

To summarize, many mainline Christians may be surprised to discover either that they are already evangelicals or are closer to being evangelicals than they realize. Those mainline Christians who are hostile to evangelicalism should consider the possibility that much of their opposition is based on misinformation, either about what being an evangelical entails or about the alleged grounds that are often thought to undermine evangelical convictions in the late twentieth century.

A WORD TO EVANGELICALS IN MAINLINE CHURCHES

Not surprisingly, evangelicals in the mainline churches differ greatly in their understanding of Christianity and the issues confronting their Church, in the depth of their spiritual lives, and in their commitment to the cause of renewal.

One of the most urgent needs of such people is greater information. Such Christians need to become better informed about the Bible as well as about the rudiments of Christian doctrine. In this regard, several fine books written at a level appropriate to laypeople are available. They include: James Packer, *Knowing God* (Downers Grove, Illinois: InterVarsity Press, 1973); John Stott, *Basic Christianity* (Grand Rapids: Eerdmans, 1957); and C. S. Lewis, *Mere Christianity* (New York: Macmillan, 1952). All of these books are available in inexpensive paperback editions.

But mainline Christians also need information about how the present theological crisis in the Church developed, about the nature of contemporary evangelicalism, and about the relationship of modern evangelicalism to earlier periods in church history. A helpful discussion of these topics can be found in the book *Evangelicals in America* by Ronald Nash (Nashville: Abingdon Press, 1987). Nash's book also contains a helpful bibliography for those interested in a further investigation of the subject.

Also important is information about current religious trends in the U.S. and the world. Such information is often available from evangelical periodicals like *Christianity Today* and *Eternity.*

Evangelicals within the mainline churches should establish contacts with the renewal movements in their denomination. They can benefit from renewal publications that discuss denominational issues from an evangelical perspective. Most of the chapters in this book tell interested parties how to contact these renewal movements and publications.

But as important as information may be, mainline evangelicals need to become active in the cause of renewal. Almost every contributor to this book has stressed the fact that renewal is a grass roots movement. It must begin with the individual believer. It must be spread to those with whom the evangelical believer has close contact. This can be done through Sunday school classes or home Bible study groups. Mainline evangelicals need to become renewal-activists. They may have to become missionaries, not only in their own local congregation, but at increasingly higher levels of their denominational structure.

While evangelical renewal must always begin with individual believers, it also requires organization. It is at this point where renewal organizations already in place may be the most help. Many renewal organizations are able to send representatives to local churches and in this way provide encouragement and support for local renewal efforts.

This is by no means a complete account of all that mainline evangelicals can or should do. But it does indicate some of the more important starting-points for the mainline evangelical who wants to begin making a contribution to the cause of renewal in his local church and in his denomination.

A WORD TO EVANGELICALS OUTSIDE THE MAINLINE CHURCHES

As things stand at present, the vast majority of evangelicals belong to nonmainline denominations. A large number of these people, especially older Christians, may have left a mainline denomination for a more conservative Church. Evangelicals outside the mainline Churches often have little interest in what goes on in the larger denominations. In some cases, they may have given up any hope for evangelical revival in these Churches. Evangelical pastors in nonmainline Churches often see themselves and their congregations in an adversarial relationship with "the liberal church" downtown.

Evangelicals outside the mainline Churches can provide helpful support for the renewal movement. This may sometimes require a change of attitude; it may sometimes require placing the advancement of God's Kingdom ahead of the advancement of their own congregation. What seems clear is that more nonmainline evangelicals need to get involved and find ways of supporting the cause of evangelical renewal.

Ronald H. Nash

NOTES

INTRODUCTION

1. For more on all this, see Ronald H. Nash, *Evangelicals in America* (Nashville: Abingdon Press, 1987).
2. Emilio Nuñez, *Liberation Theology* (Chicago: Moody, 1985), p. 37.
3. James I. Packer, *"Fundamentalism" and the Word of God* (Grand Rapids: Eerdmans, 1958), pp. 25, 26.

CHAPTER ONE

1. *Religion in Life*, Autumn 1933.
2. In J. D. Douglas and Earle A. Cairns, *The New International Dictionary of the Christian Church* (Grand Rapids: Zondervan, 1978), p. 359.
3. In David A. MacLennan, *And Are We Yet Alive?* (Lima, Ohio: CSS of Ohio, 1978), p. 9.

CHAPTER TWO

1. Deism asserts the intellectual reality or rational apprehension of God, but not a personal God involved with His creation. Such faith, while accepting the existence of the Deity, denied supernatural influences in the natural realm. Thus, miracles were given natural explanation or were dismissed out of hand. Thomas Jefferson, an Episcopalian and prominent Deist, even created his own version of the Bible in which all supernatural events had been snipped out!
2. Stephen Neill, *Anglicanism,* 4th ed. (New York: Oxford University Press, 1977), p. 191.
3. *Ibid.*
4. James Thayer Addison, *The Episcopal Church in the United States, 1789-1931* (New York: Archon Books, 1969), p. 213.
5. As Neill observes, "Evangelicals have, happily, never been a party—their inveterate habit of biting and devouring one another over microscopic differences of opinion makes it unlikely that they ever will be." He observes that evangelicals gathered in small, intense fellowships and devotional groups. Sometimes this habit promotes separation into a particular group holding a particular point of view—a sect, a branch of a larger unit that has broken away. See Neill, *Anglicanism,* pp. 237, 238.
6. Helen Smith Shoemaker, *I Stand By the Door* (Waco, Texas: Word, 1967), p. 167.

7. Samuel M. Shoemaker, *With the Holy Spirit and with Fire* (New York: Harper and Row, 1960), p. 119.

8. One reason that healing ministries help more traditional Episcopalians accept the charismatic movement may be that healing has a sacramental element to it (the sacrament of unction) in the liturgical tradition. If something is connected to sacraments in the Episcopal Church, it will have a much better and easier time being accepted in the mainstream of the Episcopal Church.

9. From the statement "Our Testimony Today," in Michael Marshall, *The Gospel Conspiracy in the Episcopal Church* (Wilton, Connecticut: Morehouse-Barlow, 1986), p. 147.

10. From "Revelation, Renewal and Reformation: A Statement of United Purpose," in *ibid.,* p. 142.

11. As referred to in *ibid.,* p. 57.

12. The Pelagian heresy stressed the perfectibility of man and man's innate goodness which can, by God's grace, work towards perfection. The distortion and subsequent heresy is the lack of seriousness about the extent of human sinfulness and man's need for grace. Pelagius was a British monk (d. 418). His sunny disposition about human nature has appealed to the reasonableness in English character and especially appealed to liberals in the nineteenth century with their view of the progress of man.

13. Ultimately the question returns to authority. Shall we accept the testimony of Scripture and the early Church about the imminent return of Christ? Or shall we draw greater conclusions from reason and tradition in this case? The evangelicals opt for Scripture.

14. The Rev. Dr. Philip Edgecombe Hughes currently is visiting professor of New Testament at Westminster Theological Seminary in Philadelphia, having served there since 1970. During that time, he also has been the professor of theology at Trinity Episcopal School for Ministry (1979-80). Prior to his service at Westminster, he was professor of historical theology at the Conwell School of Theology in Philadelphia (1968-70) and guest professor of New Testament at Columbia Theological Seminary (PCUS) (1963-68). He is the author of three books: *Christian Ethics in Secular Society, Commentary on 2 Corinthians,* and *Commentary on the Epistle to the Hebrews.*

CHAPTER THREE

1. Merton P. Strommen, et al, *A Study of Generations* (Minneapolis: Augsburg, 1972).

2. *Ibid.,* p. 106.

3. *Ibid.,* p. 367.

4. *Ibid.,* p. 108.

5. *Ibid.,* p. 379.

6. *Ibid.,* p. 369.

7. *Ibid.,* p. 296. Among other things, Pelagianism teaches that human beings are not totally dependent upon God's grace for salvation but have the ability to effect their own salvation.

8. *Ibid.,* p. 369.

9. *Ibid.,* p. 371.

10. *Ibid.*

11. For example, the views of the influential German Lutheran Rudolf Bultmann are explained and criticized in the book *Christian Faith and Historical Understanding* by Ronald Nash (Grand Rapids: Zondervan, 1984). The existentialist view of the Bible held by another deceased Lutheran, Paul Tillich, is critiqued in Ronald Nash, *The Word of God and the Mind of Man* (Grand Rapids: Zondervan, 1982).

12. Duane W. H. Arnold and C. George Fry, *The Way, The Truth and the Life: An Introduction to Lutheran Christianity* (Grand Rapids: Baker, 1982), p. 134.
13. *Ibid.*, pp. 134, 135.
14. *Ibid.*, p. 141.
15. *Book of Concord,* SC XI 632:95-96.
16. *What Luther Says,* Vol. 3 (St. Louis: Concordia, 1969), p. 1500, number 44852.
17. *Formula of Concord,* Ep., Rule and Norm.

CHAPTER FOUR

1. The split in 1947 also had roots in a long-standing dispute over the policy of the American Baptist Foreign Mission Society to send out theologically liberal missionaries.
2. Any list of Baptist distinctives would include the following: the Lordship of Jesus Christ, the supremacy of the Scriptures, the priesthood of believers, believer's baptism, regenerate church membership, separation of church and state, religious freedom, the independence of the local church, and the evangelization of the world.

CHAPTER FIVE

1. Richard G. Hutcheson, "Leaving the Mainstream," a chapter in the book, *Peacemaking? or Resistance?,* edited by Ted M. Dorman (Nashville: Presbyterians for Democracy and Religious Freedom, 1986), n.p.
2. Ervin S. Duggan, "A Church in the Political Thicket," *Public Opinion,* Summer 1986, p. 14.
3. *Ibid.*
4. *Ibid.*
5. *Ibid.*, p. 10.
6. *Ibid.*, p. 11.
7. *Ibid.*
8. *Ibid.*, p. 14.
9. Dana M. Wilbanks and Ronald H. Stone, *Presbyterians and Peacemaking: Are We Now Called to Resistance?* (New York: Advisory Council on Church and Society, 1985).
10. Ted M. Dorman, *Peacemaking? or Resistance?* (Nashville: Presbyterians for Democracy and Religious Freedom, 1986).
11. Welde's comments appear in the article "Bridges and Rising Tides," by Randy Peterson, *The Presbyterian Communique,* Spring 1986.
12. The sources for this and earlier uncredited quotations are official publications of PUBC.
13. This list was compiled by Rev. Matthew Welde.

CHAPTER SIX

1. Lester G. McAllister and William E. Tucker, *Journey in Faith* (St. Louis: The Bethany Press, 1975), p. 362.
2. Herbert L. Willett, *The Bible Through The Centuries* (Chicago: Willet, Clark, & Colby Publishers, 1929), p. 289.
3. W. A. Welsh, "What Restructure Means to Me," *Midstream,* Vol. 3 (September 1963), pp. 101, 102.
4. These numbers do not include the loss of churches and the membership of those churches after the 1968 restructuring of the Church.

5. Garrett, *op. cit.*, p. 724.
6. Joseph A. Garshaw, "Concerns About the Church," *Disciple Renewal*, Spring 1986, p. 1.
7. Donald McGavran, "The Essential Element in Renewal," *Disciple Renewal*, January 1986, p. 1.
8. Herbert Miller, "Will Disciples Reverse Their Death March?," to be published in Fall 1986, *Disciple Renewal*.
9. Additional information about the renewal organizations discussed in this section may be found at the end of the chapter.
10. Doug Harvey, "The Centrality of the Bible," *Disciple Renewal*, January 1986, p. 3.
11. Donald McGavran, from a pamphlet entitled "I Accuse! I Plead!," distributed by the Continuing Christian Churches Movement. McGavran is a member of the CCCM Board.

CHAPTER SEVEN

1. The Board of Directors of the UCPBW uncovered evidence that suggested strongly that persons holding orthodox or evangelical convictions were being screened out of Synod delegations at the conference levels of the Church.
2. The text of The Dubuque Declaration appears at the end of this chapter.
3. To get even more specific, point two was intended to oppose views associated with liberation theology and process theology.
4. Barbara Weller served as interim executive director until Mr. Sanders could resign his parish and relocate. An attorney, Larry Wood, was elected as the new president of the Board of Directors.

CHAPTER EIGHT

1. *L'Osservatore Romano*, June 30, 1977.
2. The Cursillo movement is an evangelistic movement that began in Spain after World War II and spread to Latin America and, to a lesser degree, to the U.S. Focolare is a communitarian movement that originated in Italy during the war and has grown chiefly in Europe, South America, and Africa. Communion and Liberation *(Comunione e Liberazione)* is an Italian movement with spiritual, intellectual, and political dimensions.

CONCLUSION

1. For recent discussions of some of the issues involved in all this, see Ronald Nash, *The Word of God and the Mind of Man* (Grand Rapids: Zondervan, 1982); Ronald Nash, *Christian Faith and Historical Understanding* (Grand Rapids: Zondervan, 1983); Ronald Nash, *The Concept of God* (Grand Rapids: Zondervan, 1983); and Ronald Nash, *Christianity and the Hellenistic World* (Grand Rapids: Zondervan, 1984).
2. For more on this, see Ronald Nash, *Evangelicals in America* (Nashville: Abingdon Press, 1987), Chapter 8.
3. Worth reading in this regard are Ronald Nash, *Poverty and Wealth* (Westchester, Illinois: Crossway, 1986) and Ronald Nash, *Social Justice and the Christian Church* (Grand Rapids: Baker, 1987).